"It's your thoughts behind the words you speak that create your attitude."

— *Jeffrey Gitomer*

Positive attitude is defined as

The way you dedicate yourself to the way you think.

The definition for a negative attitude is exactly the same.

This book is dedicated to the way you think.

Jeffrey Gitomer's

LITTLE GOLD BOOK of

YES!

Attitude

How to Find, Build, and Keep
a YES! Attitude for a Lifetime of
SUCCESS

FT Press

Little Gold Book of YES! Attitude

© 2007 Pearson Education, Inc. Publishing as FT Press
Upper Saddle River, New Jersey 07458.
Vice President and Editor-in-Chief: Tim Moore.

To order additional copies of this title, contact your local bookseller or call 704/333-1112.
The author may be contacted at the following address:
BuyGitomer
310 Arlington Ave., Loft 329
Charlotte, NC 28203
Phone: 704/333-1112 Fax: 704/333-1011
E-mail: salesman@gitomer.com
Web sites: www.gitomer.com, www.trainone.com

Edited by Jessica McDougall.
Page design by Mike Wolff.
Cover design by Josh Gitomer.
Photography by Mitchell Kearney.

Printed in China by RR Donnelley.

Fifth printing, March 2009

Library of Congress Cataloging-in-Publication Data

Gitomer, Jeffrey H.
   Jeffrey Gitomer's little gold book of yes! attitude : how to find, build and keep a yes! attitude for a lifetime of success.
      p. cm.
   ISBN 978-0-13-198647-3 (hardback : alk. paper)
      1. Attitude (Psychology) 2. Change (Psychology) 3. Optimism. 4. Success–Psychological aspects. 5. Happiness–Psychological aspects. 6. Work–Psychological aspects. I. Title. II. Title: Little gold book of yes! attitude.

   BF327.G58 2007
   158.1--dc22

                                                            2006031190

"We lift ourselves by our thought. If you want to enlarge your life, you must first enlarge your thought of it and of yourself. Hold the ideal of yourself as you long to be, always everywhere."

Orison Swett Marden 1850-1924
Author and founder of *Success* magazine

"To think you can, creates the force that can."

Orison Swett Marden
From his book *Victorious Attitude,* 1916

"At the beginning of any task, more than anything else, your attitude will affect its successful outcome."

Jeffrey Gitomer
Author. Speaker. Salesman.

The subtle difference between a positive attitude and a *YES!*Attitude

Both are GREAT, but *YES!* is a bit more powerful because it assumes that everything you say and do will start with "*YES!*" even when it's "No."

A *YES!*Attitude helps you formulate your responses in a positive form.

A *YES!*Attitude is more declarative. It tells people – in a word – that their expectation will be met and that your answer to whatever they want or need will be "*YES!*" or in a positive format.

Everyone wants to hear "*YES!*" And if you think of yourself as a *YES!* person, not only will you be in a positive frame of mind, but you will also have positive expectations.

This book is about *both* positive attitude and *YES!*Attitude. Not just what they are – it also defines insights, game plans, and actions for attitude achievement. You will learn how to keep your *YES!*Attitude forever *and* how to pass it on to those you love.

CAUTION:
Attitude is hokey

One of the reasons so few people study positive attitude is because they read about it and think it's silly. It's not silly, it's hokey.

The difference between silly and hokey is: silly is silly, hokey is valid.

Throughout this book, I am going to share with you the quotes of other masters of attitude that have influenced me.

If you think they are silly, now would be a good time to give this book to somebody else. But keep tabs on who you give the book to. *They'll be the ones who become successful later in life* while you're still grumbling.

If you read old books on attitude (the two most dominant of which are *Think and Grow Rich* and *How to Win Friends & Influence People*), you will find that they are hokey. But hokey also means easy to read and easy to understand. The hard part is application. You may think the ideas are too hokey to apply. But that's the secret: They're not only hokey, they're totally simple and totally easy to apply and master with practice.

How to benefit from this book

This book is divided into 5.5 elements. Each element is designed for a specific purpose. Each element builds on another and creates a total awareness and game plan for you to **understand**, **apply**, **become proficient at**, and finally, **master and maintain your attitude**.

It's an understanding and a game plan. *All you have to do is read and take action.* Daily.

Realize that it took you years to screw up your attitude. Give yourself a few hours to read and discover *why* and *how to fix it forever*.

*"I know I should stop whining and complaining...
but it's taken me years to get this good at it!"*

Watch out for the AHA!

As you are reading, at some point there will be an **AHA!** Maybe it's in the area of associations or influences, maybe it's taking the test, or maybe it's just the exposure to the information. But it will occur. And when it does, that's not *the* beginning of attitude awareness, it's *your* beginning of attitude awareness.

And…**Watch out for the trademark.** I have trademarked the phrase *YES!Attitude* and will be creating more books, classroom courses, online courses, and helpful products ad infinitum.

I am telling you this for 2.5 reasons:

1. GET PERMISSION FIRST. You must get my authorization to use the phrase *YES!Attitude* in any of your writing or training.

2. YOUR OPPORTUNITY TO BE A LEARNING PARTNER. I have classroom and online courses for individuals and corporations. Just call 704/333-1112, or e-mail yes@gitomer.com.

2.5 YOUR OPPORTUNITY TO BE A PROFIT PARTNER. If you have a great idea that I have not already put into practice, I am more than willing to share it (and any revenues that might accrue from it) with others.

Please understand that the spirit and purpose of this book is to help you achieve your *YES!Attitude*. When you do, it will help you in every aspect of your business life and your personal life. And that's an **AHA!** that you can take to the bank.

Got attitude?
How do you get a positive attitude?

Study attitude, think attitude, and express attitude every day.

I have 982 books in my library on the subjects of positive mental attitude and personal development. All of them address the importance of and the benefits derived from positive thinking. Most of them don't have a game plan that you can embrace and implement to achieve your own positive attitude. That's why this book is in your hands.

As with all opportunities, you have a choice. I will give you the thoughts and tools you need to achieve your own personal positive attitude and your own *YES!Attitude* forever.

BUT, it's not up to me to do your work.

My biggest hope is that you will seize the opportunity to wake up every morning as the happiest person on the face of this planet, even if your roof caved in on you while you were asleep.

> *"After my house burned down,*
> *I saw the moon more clearly."*

– Old Zen saying
(and a *YES!Attitude* expression)

How many attitude lessons and courses have you had?
None? Or not enough?

If 100% of your success is tied to your attitude when listening, communicating, serving customers, and doing your job, then how come you've never taken a course in it?

You're holding in your hands
your first lesson.

The entire formula – everything you
need to start on the positive path and stay
there – regardless of outside circumstances.

I'm not going to say anything silly like, "Welcome to the first day of your new success life."

But I *am* going to say that your old life hasn't been a bed of positive attitude roses. And dare to say, that when you've run your hand up and down those roses, occasionally you've run into a prick.

OUCH!

"Jeffrey, will I have a positive attitude when I'm done reading this book?"

Unless you had one before
you started reading it…

BUT you will have a *better* attitude.

AND this book has the simple answers
that will put you on the path to a lifelong
positive attitude, a **YES!Attitude**, that will
pull you through any personal or career
challenge and propel you to the top of the
ladder when things are normal.

All you have to do is apply a little
self-discipline and follow a few principles.

THIS BOOK *CANNOT*

I can tell you and show you how I did it, but in the end, you can't just read it. You gotta study it, project it, cut it out, carry it with you, post it, think it, speak it, and live it – every minute of every day.

You can't gain a positive attitude by reading a book.

You can gain insight, you can gain knowledge from the lessons in the exercises, and you can practice and implement.

You can't gain the self-discipline and the thought process by reading a book.

Those will have to come from you.

I cannot change your self-discipline or your thought patterns, but I can teach you the lessons. I cannot change the way you respond to your circumstances, but I can make you think about them to a point where you may take some action for yourself.

THIS BOOK *CAN*

Inspire you.
Show you where you are.
Spoon-feed you actions and ideas.
Give you attitude answers.

BUT, I can't change your attitude – I can only create an atmosphere so you can change it yourself.

Read it *today.*
Study it *tomorrow.*
Practice it *daily.*
Keep it *forever.*
Refer to it *often.*

If someone wants to borrow this book, buy them one.

And go to the GitBit box on my Web site (www.gitomer.com) each time you are prompted. When you go, you'll receive additional, free, **YES!Attitude** information.

I promise

PROMISE 1: Once you begin to take these actions, make the right choices, and create the right responses, you will be on the road to achieving the right attitude. First a positive attitude, then a **YES!Attitude**.

PROMISE 2: Once these attitude actions, responses, and choices become a way of life, then you will be on the ever-continuing path of maintaining your **YES!Attitude**.

PROMISE 2.5: I'm going to give you the insight and awareness. I'm going to give you the attributes and the understanding. But *you* have to take the actions, and *you* have to create the reactions, every day.

"Your attitude is thinning. I've hired the best surgeon in the city to give you an attitude transplant!"

Jeffrey Gitomer's
LITTLE GOLD BOOK *of*

Table of Contents

Expanded Table of Contents

ELEMENT ONE   INSIGHT TO YOUR INSIDE ATTITUDE

ELEMENT TWO ATTITUDE SELF AWARENESS

ELEMENT THREE ATTITUDE ACTIONS

ELEMENT FOUR ATTITUDE ATTRIBUTES

ELEMENT FIVE ATTITUDE ACHIEVEMENT

YES! Attitude

INSIGHT
TO YOUR
INSIDE ATTITUDE

Your humor, your internal belief system, your desire to be good, better, best, your ability to process thoughts and respond, your ability to harmonize with others, your ability to understand your senses, your ability to look at things from a different perspective...
the **YES!** perspective.

How important is positive attitude to success?

1

ATTITUDE IS EVERYTHING

— AND —

ATTITUDE IS THE FOUNDATION FOR EVERYTHING

Where does positive attitude come from?

Positive attitude comes from within.

Positive attitude has nothing to do with what happens to you. It's what you do with, and how you react to, what happens to you.

Positive attitude comes from your ability to process thoughts in a positive way, regardless of the circumstance. And it's never 100%. That's why, in spite of your determination to be positive at every moment, you'll have highs and lows based on your thought process and your vulnerability to others.

HERE'S THE GOOD NEWS: The more you work on your attitude, the less vulnerable you become to the negative aspect of it.

The most interesting aspect of attitude is that "instant" only applies to the negative part. Someone can make you angry (negative) in a second, but it can take years to achieve the positive. Positive attitude comes from your own thought process combined with your determination to stay in the right frame of mind. It ain't easy to get there, but it's worth it once you do.

THE *YES!* FACTOR

Picture in your mind the feeling of crossing the finish line first, or winning a ball game, or completing some big task, or making a sale, and at the end making some gesture of triumph, like raising your fists in the air and screaming, "*YES!*"

Can you picture it? It's a happy moment, it's a joyous moment, it's a triumphant moment, it's a winning moment, it's a positive moment, and that's why you scream "*YES!*" Wouldn't it be cool if every moment of your life was like that? So, what's preventing it? **BIGGEST ANSWER**: You!

The reason that *YES!* is easier to understand than positive is that *YES!* is an experience that you've had many times. You won the race, you got the raise, your team won the game, you landed the client, and you screamed, "*YES!*"

A large part of attitude achievement is the visualization. It's easier to visualize *YES!* than it is to visualize positive. When something great happens, no one screams, "Positive!" Everyone screams, "*YES!*" That's the difference. That's the *YES!* factor.

Free Git✗Bit: You've been screaming *YES!* all your life. **Need to jog your memory of those *I did it* moments?** Go to www.gitomer.com, register if you are a first-time user, and enter the words I DID IT in the GitBit box.

There is nothing new about attitude…except yours

Positive attitude has been preached since the Bible. Every major philosopher, every major theologian, and especially every major personal development expert has preached the virtue of positive thought, positive action, and positive attitude for centuries. Millions of words have been written (and rewritten) on the subject.

You would think that, with all this information at their fingertips, everyone (you included) would have a positive attitude. You would be thinking wrong.

You can read and listen all you want, but unless you *decide* that you want to become a positive person, a person who thinks positive, acts positive, and speaks positive (both proactive and reactive), your attitude will not be a positive one.

What *is* new is your opportunity to begin your dedication to your attitude as you read this book.

And, of course, you immediately want to know, "What's in this for me?"

Well, Sparky, that's a negative thought. Why not think, "Hey, if I'm able to get a positive attitude and a **YES!Attitude** as a result of reading, studying, and applying the principles of this book, look at all the wonderful things that will happen to me."

You'll feel better about yourself, your loved ones, your co-workers, your friends, your job, your career, and your life. You'll see choices more clearly, and you'll create an attraction both from people, and for luck, that will never go away.

But FIRST, you have to "get it." And that requires **STUDY**, **WORK**, and **DEDICATION**.

I gained a *YES!***Attitude** when I was 26. Thirty-four years later, I still have it. It is at the core of my being, and it can be at yours, too.

All it takes is that one **AHA!**, and a whole new way of thinking will open up for you.

Once you discover that attitude is yours for the taking, you have to study it (from other experts), expose yourself to it (from positive things and people), and practice it (from your soul) until you "get it." Not just "understand" it, immerse yourself in it for awhile until it's part of your being, inside your body and mind, and you become "at one" with your attitude.

And then, it's a lifelong dedication to renewing the process daily. But that process is a joy. A short daily renewal of affirmation, or reading in the morning, is all it takes.

ATTITUDE IS A GIFT – one you give yourself.
ATTITUDE IS A BLESSING – one you give yourself.

Once you have a positive attitude, you bless yourself and others who come in contact with you, forever.

That's what's in it for you, Sparky.

What is a positive attitude?

The simple definition is *the way you dedicate yourself to the way you think.* Interestingly, it's also the definition of a negative attitude.

The more complex definition is *how you choose to dedicate yourself to the way you think, how you choose to dedicate yourself to being positive, and how you choose to dedicate yourself to reacting in a positive way.* And your choice must be consistent.

Most people have a positive attitude some of the time. This means some people have a negative attitude all the time. Few people have a positive attitude all the time. And you know who the positive people are. They're evident by the way they conduct themselves and the way they respond to things.

But let's get back to you, because in the end, that's who you really care about anyway. Positive is a state of mind, and all the things that surround positive can either reinforce it, challenge it, or destroy it. That's another choice.

What choices have you made, and what is reinforcing you?

Attitude challenges are everywhere, and the closer they are to you, the more vulnerable you become. Parents, siblings, spouses, and close friends all influence your thinking. Often, their problems become your problems. Often, their life's crap becomes your life's crap. And often, their pity party sends you an engraved invitation and, like a fool, you accept it.

Me? I walk away. I don't pity people in the pity party. I focus on me. (I guess if I had to describe their party in one word, it would be the obvious: pitiful.)

Me? I study attitude every day. It reinforces my automatic positive thinking.

Me? I look for how I can take a situation and turn it into a win – even if it means jumping into the middle of the negative, battling a little bit, and emerging in the positive.

One of the biggest mistakes people make with their attitude is leaving a situation angry or grumbling. Big mistake. Employees not talking to one another over petty issues, spouses using words of hatred that they can never take back, and reactions to confrontational situations that are left in a negative state.

Think about the last few heated exchanges that you've had. What was your response to the situation? How did you leave the situation? Dissect that, and you'll have a clearer view of where your attitude is, and how much distance there is between yours and a positive one.

Is there a formula? Of course there's a formula. But the formula, like many other elements of attitude, is hokey. And on the surface the formula seems way too simple to be the driver of something so important as your attitude. I'll give it to you later in the book when it's time to take action.

But let me give you a hint about the formula from an old attitude quote by Aldous Huxley, "It's not what happens to you, it's what you do with what happens to you."

Introducing the most important person in the world
Hint: It ain't the customer

In every one of my seminars, I select one person and ask, "Bill, when you're speaking with your biggest customer, who is the most important person in the world?" Ninety-nine percent of the time, the person I selected will answer, "The customer."

"Really?" I say. "Suppose there were two people left on the planet, you and the big customer, and one of them had to die. Who do you want to see drop dead?"

"The customer!" says Bill.

"So, we've now established that **you**, Bill, are the most important person in the world. But the problem is, when you're speaking with a big customer, they think that **they** are the most important person in the world."

You can take the word "customer" and substitute mother, father, sister, brother, friend, or teacher. Everyone *feels as though* they are the most important person in the world, or *wants to feel* that *they* are the most important person in the world. Your job is to treat them that way. And your positive attitude permits that action.

This is real easy to understand in business. It's called customer service, or helping. In families and other personal relationships, it's a bit more delicate. These are people who you will be with forever (or at least at one time thought you would be). This is where your attitude can affect the quality of the relationship bit by bit over time. It will either go up, go down, or stay the same based on your attitude and your responses to the situations that you encounter.

Everyone *wants* to be positive, and many people even *think* that they are positive, but they aren't. They act it in terms of what will serve themselves best, rather than serving others best.

A large part of getting your attitude from negative to positive and from positive to *YES!* is phrasing responses in terms of the other person NOT in terms of yourself.

The secret of a positive attitude is being selfish *on the inside* (the way you think about yourself, the personal pride that you have, the person you seek to become, and your thoughts just before you respond or take action) and then helping or serving others because you feel good enough about yourself to help them.

Once you get the fact that positive attitude is all about you *on the inside* (your thoughts about your actions and responses), you've made the first breakthrough.

Once you have that realization, once you get that first breakthrough, then it's time to *turn the page*.

"Keep in mind, YOU are the greatest!"

Understanding that you are the most important person in the world is a key step in the direction of *YES!* Attitude.

– *Jeffrey Gitomer*

Positive attitude is ATTRACTIVE and CONTAGIOUS

People are attracted to others (or not) based on attitude. And positive attitude is contagious. You can give it to others. But understand that you create the basis of it and you create the foundation for it by your thoughts and actions at the beginning of every day.

Positive attitude is the foundation for EVERYTHING.

- **It's the mood you're in when you wake up in the morning.**

- **It's the mood you're in when you walk into the bathroom in the morning and look in the mirror.**

- **It's the mood you're in when you talk to your spouse.**

- **It's the mood you're in when you talk to your kids.**

- **It's the mood you're in when you drive to work.**

- **It's the mood you're in when you get to work.**

- It's the mood you're in when you talk to your co-workers.

- It's the mood you're in when you talk with your boss.

- It's the mood you're in when you talk to your customers.

What kind of mood are you always in? Attitude is not about always being moody – attitude is about always being in a great mood. In the '70s, there was a fad product called a "mood ring." Everybody bought one, except me.

I already knew my mood: **Great!** And I've been in a great mood ever since. If you have to check your mood, it probably means you have to check your attitude.

"When I'm feeling positive, my mood ring turns green.
When I'm angry, it's orange. When I'm depressed, it's blue.
Today it's plaid. I guess I'm in the mood for anything!"

Everyone is born happy, but it takes years to figure that out

Positive attitude happens. **NO!**

Positive attitude happens when you *think* it will happen. Positive attitude happens when you *make* it happen.

You acquire your attitude over time. It's based on your family, your environment, your friends, and the things you expose yourself to. It's also based on your experiences in school, with friends, on jobs, and the other episodes that constitute your life.

The lesson here is pretty obvious: If you grew up in an unhappy household, where your parents put you down, it would have been a struggle for you to be a happy person.

Internal happiness is the beginning of positive attitude, not the achievement of it.

Some people (hopefully you) will grasp the fact that all of the attributes you need to achieve your *YES!*Attitude are already inside of you. They may have been suppressed for years in the form of negativity, but all you have to do is change your focus and your outlook, and your *YES!*Attitude will follow.

YOU'LL BEGIN TO REALIZE:

- **Attitude is your choice, not your circumstance.**

- **Attitude is the way you respond to the situation, not the situation itself.**

- **You have control over the way you choose, and the way you respond.**

Attitude is not something that you can understand in one read. Reread the last 15 pages until you're certain you have a firm understanding of where the balance lies between negative, positive, and ***YES!***

"A butterfly is a caterpillar with a positive attitude!"

Do you have a positive attitude?

Building attitude insight and awareness are the first steps in building a positive attitude. But most people take the words "positive attitude" for granted. They've never exposed themselves to the root elements of a positive attitude, nor have they challenged themselves to discover what causes it.

I bet every one of you thinks you have a positive attitude. And the same number of you have NEVER taken a course in it. Congratulations, you're in the big club.

LET'S GO A BIT DEEPER: How much of your success is dependent on your positive attitude? The answer is somewhere between "lots" and "all," or 80-100%.

So, 80-100% of your success is dependent on your positive attitude. Yet, you've had no formal training?

Suppose you need surgery and I recommend a surgeon with no formal training, but he "thinks" he can do a great job. Get it?

Everyone says they have a positive attitude, but less than one in one hundred actually does! **One percent.** Are you in the one percentile? All you have to do is take this simple test...

Attitude self-test

What is your definition of a positive attitude?

My definition of a positive attitude is _____

_____

_____

What percentage of your success is dependent on your positive attitude?

NOTE: You may put up to 100% in each category. Your total can be up to 400%.

When listening	_60_ %
When communicating	_100_ %
When serving customers	_90_ %
When doing your job	_100_ %
Total	_350_ %

What is your rating of your positive attitude?

1   **2**   **3**   **4**   **5**   **⑥**   **7**   **8**   **9**   **10**

is worst   is greatest

Does your attitude set the tone for the people you deal with?

● *YES!* ○ No

How many hours of positive attitude training did you get...

In grade school	____	○ None
In high school	____	○ None
In college	____	○ None
At work	____	○ None

"Look at it this way, you've got no place to go but UP!"

Part One

HOW TO TAKE THIS TEST: Carefully circle the number on the right that represents your present situation.

1=All the time or daily 2=Frequently 3=Sometimes 4=Rarely 5=Never

☐	I watch the news.	1	2	3	④	5
☐	I talk about the news.	1	2	③	4	5
☐	I am affected by, or talk about, bad weather.	1	2	3	④	5
☐	I am mad at someone for more than one hour.	1	②	3	4	5
☐	When something goes wrong, I blame others.	1	2	③	4	5
☐	When something goes wrong, I dwell on self-blame.	1	②	3	4	5
☐	I bring my problems to work.	1	2	3	④	5
☐	I talk about my problems at work.	1	2	3	④	5
☐	I take my work problems home.	1	2	③	4	5

Part Two

READ CLOSELY: The numeric values reverse in this part.

1=Never 2=Rarely 3=Sometimes 4=Frequently 5=All the time

☐ I am an enthusiastic person. 1 2 ③ ④ 5

☐ I am happy on the inside. 1 2 ③ 4 5

☐ I look for the good in things. 1 2 ③ 4 5

☐ I usually talk about
the good in things. 1 2 ③ 4 5

☐ I say why I like things
and people, not why I don't. 1 2 3 ④ 5

☐ I look for the opportunity when
something bad happens. 1 2 3 ④ 5

☐ I forgive people who have
hurt or offended me. 1 ② 3 4 5

☐ If I have nothing nice to
say, I say nothing. 1 2 3 ④ 5

☐ I encourage myself. 1 2 3 ④ 5

☐ I use positive-attitude language. I avoid can't and won't. 1 2 ③ 4 5

☐ I have a positive self-image. 1 2 3 ④ 5

☐ I exercise choices that build my positive attitude. 1 2 ③ 4 5

☐ I help others without expectation or measuring. 1 ② 3 4 5

☐ I am more motivated to help people than I am to make money. 1 2 ③ 4 5

☐ I often encourage others to succeed. 1 2 ③ 4 5

☐ I am happy about myself and my life. 1 2 ③ 4 5

☐ I work on my attitude every day. 1 ② 3 4 5

☐ I listen to attitude audio tapes and I attend seminars. 1 ② 3 4 5

☐ I ignore people who try to discourage me or tell me "you can't." 1 2 ③ 4 5

☐ I count my blessings every day. 1 2 3 ④ 5

☐ I believe in myself. 1 2 ③ 4 5

Attitude scorecard

HERE'S HOW TO CALCULATE YOUR SCORE: First, count the number of 1s that you circled in Part One and put them on the line on the following page next to 1× under Part One. Then count the number of 2s that you circled in Part One and put them on the line next to 2×. After that, count the number of 3s that you circled and put them on the line next to 3×. Do the same for your 4s and 5s. Repeat this process for Part Two.

To calculate your total, multiply the left (1×, 2×) number by your number.

Then, add your numbers from the right-hand columns to get your **Part ONE Total Score** and your **Part TWO Total Score**. Finally, add your **Part ONE Total Score** and your **Part TWO Total Score** to get your **TOTAL SCORE**.

FOR EXAMPLE: In Part One, if you selected 2 for four of the points, 4 for two of the points, and 5 for three of the points, you would have a 4 on the 2× line, a 2 on the 4× line, a 3 on the 5× line, and a 0 on all other lines in the left column. Then, multiplying across, you would get $(1 \times 0 = 0)+(2 \times 4 = 8)+(4 \times 2 = 8)+(5 \times 3 = 15)$. By adding all the numbers down the right-hand column (0+8+0+8+15=31), you would get a **Part ONE Total Score** of 31.

Part One

1 × _0_ = _____
2 × _2_ = _4_
3 × _3_ = _9_
4 × _4_ = _16_
5 × _0_ = _____

Part ONE Total Score _29_

Part Two

1 × _0_ = _0_
2 × _4_ = _8_
3 × _11_ = _33_
4 × _7_ = _28_
5 × _0_ = _0_

Part TWO Total Score _69_

TOTAL SCORE _98_

How positive is your attitude?

135-150   You've got a **positive attitude**! You are the greatest because you think you are.

120-134   You've got a good attitude and understand what it will take to improve. Go for the gold!

75-119   You're in the big club of people who *think* they have a positive attitude, but don't. You're in need of skill-building help and must actively work on attitude exercises every day.

50-74   You've got a negative attitude. You should read several books on attitude (in addition to this one). You need to change your work and personal habits as part of your skill building. Don't give up!

29-49   You've got to work twice as hard as the group above.

How to personalize this test (and improve)

There were 30 total statements. *Go back and check the box to the left of any statement that you scored a 1 or 2 on in Part One or a 1,2, or 3 in Part Two*. Those are your weak attitude areas. The checked boxes become you personalized game plan to get a more positive attitude. Now, all you have to do is take daily, positive action.

How'd you like your results?

Are you in the big club?

People tell me they have to watch the daily news to "keep current." My definition of "keep current" is "stay negative." All news is negative. Constant exposure to daily negative news can't possibly have a positive impact on your life. The Internet will give you all the news you need, in about a minute and a half. That will free up time that you can devote to yourself and your positive attitude.

THINK ABOUT IT THIS WAY: If you watch the news an hour a day, that's 15 full 24-hour days of negative each year.

1. How important is the news to your success?
2. What can you do with that time to build YOUR LIFE, instead of your storehouse of useless knowledge?

Do you affect the news, or does it affect you? This is a key phrase to determine whether something will positively impact you. If you can't affect it in some way or another, the best thing to do is stay away from it.

Free Git✗Bit: **Want to discover more about the YOU aspect of positive attitude?** Go to www.gitomer.com, register if you are a first-time user, and enter the words YOUYOU in the GitBit box.

1

Once you discover what your attitude is, or isn't, you'll have a starting point and an understanding of how to move forward.

Negative occurrences (like arguments) block positive and creative thought

Ever have an argument with someone and five minutes later thought to yourself, *Man, I wish I would've said (insert the perfect comeback here) to that jerk?*

Sure you have! Everyone has. The reason you couldn't think of this snappy response in the heat of the argument is that arguments are negative, and negative blocks creative thought.

Negative occurrences, thoughts, and energy are (unfortunately) much more powerful than positive thought.

It takes twice as much energy to be negative than to be positive. That's why, at the end of the argument, you may be tired.

Understand that negative energy and negative thoughts **BLOCK** positive thoughts and creative thoughts from occurring.

1

Negative people are worse than negative occurrences.

The argument is over in ten minutes – the person may hang around for years.

– Jeffrey Gitomer

The bridge between positive and negative

In business, most people focus on what *can't* get done rather than on what *can* get done. They handicap themselves mentally by telling themselves, "I can't get the guy on the phone. No one will return my call. No one will hire me. I overslept. I forgot. I didn't write it down. No one told me." And then they go into excuse mode by saying, "I didn't have enough time." Or pathetically, "I am doing the best I can."

Think about how you'd feel if someone brought you the same circumstances that you're whining about. Would you want to listen, or would you want to avoid this person at all costs? That answer is obvious. But there's a better answer, and it lies in your ability "To be, or not to be" positive. (That is the question.) If you focus on negative, the results will likely be negative. If you focus on positive anticipation and positive outcome, then positive results will follow.

Here are 7.5 on-the-job things you can do to keep the focus, intensity, drive, and commitment necessary to change your direction from "Woe is me," to "Whoa, what a life!":

1. Stop blaming circumstances for your situation. It's not the rain, or the car, or the phone, or the product. It's YOU. You have a choice in everything you do. Choose a better way. Don't blame the path – change the path. Don't blame the situation – change the situation.

2. Stop blaming other people for your situation. Take responsibility for yourself and your actions. If you are consistently blaming other people, *guess what, Bubba*, get over it – it ain't them.

3. Know your customer or prospect better. Knowing your customer is just as powerful to prevent problems as it is to handle them. If you can't get the prospect on the phone, it's your fault for not knowing the best time to reach him. Know the right time to call. Know when a decision is to be made. Double confirm every commitment.

4. Persist until you gain an answer. A prospect will respect a tenacious salesperson. If it takes 5-10 exposures to make a sale, do you have what it takes to hang in there? Even if it's "No," at least you know where you stand.

5. Know where you are or where you should be. Manage your time. Have lunch with a customer, not a friend. Keep perfect records. Know enough about your prospect or customer that follow-up becomes easy and fun. Are you organized enough to get to the tenth exposure and have the situation under control enough to make the sale?

6. Work on your skills every day. Books, CDs, seminars. You can never read enough books or listen to enough CDs. I challenge you to do it for an hour a day. One hour a day, seven days a week, for one year is equal to more than nine full weeks of work. The next time you mindlessly turn on the TV, think about what you could be doing to improve your focus and knowledge base.

7. Become solution-oriented. Instead of griping or wallowing in your problems, why not spend the same amount of time working on solutions? Being solution-oriented has done more for me and my path to success than any single strategy. Every obstacle presents an opportunity – if you're looking for it. If you're too busy concentrating on the problem, the opportunity will pass you by.

7.5 Think before talking. People speak without thinking, only to regret what they said. Every time you are about to engage someone else, think quickly about what it is you are about to say. How will the words be received? And what else could you be saying that might create a more positive expression? The goal is a positive response or result. The action seems simple, but it requires the most self-discipline. Try it a few times. You'll be amazed at the results.

ATTITUDE OPPORTUNITY: You've been given a bag of cement and a bucket of water. You can either build a stumbling block (a concrete barrier), or a stepping stone (a bridge to wherever you want to go).

The choice is (and always has been) yours. Are you missing opportunities because you are too focused on obstacles?

Free Git Bit: Why did the chicken cross the George Washington Bridge? To find out, go to www.gitomer.com, register if you are a first-time user, and enter the word CHICKEN in the GitBit box.

YES! Attitude

ATTITUDE SELF AWARENESS

AN ATTITUDE LESSON

Your self-awareness
is a combination of your
internal attention and your focus.

Attitude self-awareness
is how you think and
how you think about yourself
(most important person in the world).

Think about it in terms of your personal wisdom

Understand *yourself* **FIRST** so that you can understand and respond to others **SECOND**. That awareness will lead you to a path of understanding that the fulcrum point of how you react and respond comes from your inner thought.

And if you think about it, and you focus on it, you can transform your attitude from negative to positive, and from positive to **YES!**, just by changing the way you think.

"First seek to understand, then be understood." Everyone thinks that's a quote from Steven Covey since it's one of his *Seven Habits*. But if you go back and research, you'll find it was first spoken by Saint Francis of Assisi in the 1200's.

Both of them had it backward. St Francis, because it was 1200. Who knew anything back then? Covey, because he copied it, rather than created it.

If you don't understand yourself, how the hell can you understand someone else? If you're not aware of who you are, the barrier to understanding others is a 50-feet high, 50-feet thick, brick wall.

Your self-understanding is your personal wisdom. Once you have it, you can use it in a positive way.

Be aware of the senses that can affect your attitude

Can your attitude be linked to your senses?

Think about negative senses. These are senses that negatively affect your attitude and steer you away from success. And, believe it or not, most of us carry all these negative senses.

You have all these little negativities running around in your mind getting in the way of the positive ones. The negative senses (just like the negative thoughts) **BLOCK** your ability to focus on the positive senses – the ones that breed success.

Every negative sense has a remedy and a counter-balancing positive sense to replace it with. In my *Little Red Book of Sales Answers* (page 21–22), I present a list of negative senses with the counter-balancing positive senses that go with them.

NOW IT'S TIME TO RATE YOURSELF: As you read each negative sense, rate how the fear negatively affects or positively affects you by putting a number from one to ten next to each one. Ten is bad in the negative list. Ten is *YES!* in the positive list.

NOTE: There's no right or wrong and no pass or fail in this exercise. It's a self-awareness exercise to help you understand where you are so that you can better understand where to improve and where to grow.

Here are the negative senses:

___   **1.** I have a sense of fear.

___   **2.** I have a sense of nervousness.

___   **3.** I have a sense of rejection.

___   **4.** I have a sense of procrastination or reluctance.

___   **5.** I have a sense of justification or rationale.

___   **6.** I have a sense of self-doubt.

___   **7.** I have a sense of uncertainty.

___   **8.** I have a sense of doom.

___   **8.5** I have a sense of "I'm unlucky."

Here are the counter-balancing positive senses:

___   **1.** I have a sense of confidence.

___   **2.** I have a sense of positive anticipation.

___   **3.** I have a sense of determination.

___   **4.** I have a sense of achievement.

___   **5.** I have a sense of winning.

___   **6.** I have a sense of success.

___   **7.** I have a sense of "I'm certain."

___   **8.** I have a sense of "sunny day."

___   **8.5** I have a sense of good fortune.

I know that! vs.
How good am I at that?

2

You already know everything.

THE REALITY IS: You're not doing it.

In the previous self-evaluation of senses, there was not one sense – either positive or negative – that you didn't already know. As you read them, you mentally shook your head, "Yep, I know it. Yep, I know it."

But when you rated yourself from one to ten for each of the senses, you gained the reality of the gap between *knowing* and *mastering*.

It's the same with positive attitude.
It's the same with *YES!*Attitude.

As you transfer your thought process from understanding and awareness to action and application, you must also change your thought process from, "I know that!" to "How good am I at that?" Or better stated, "How can I become the master of that?"

Once you have formed the habit of thinking, "How good am I at that?" you will have taken one more powerful step toward your *YES!*Attitude.

People who are cocky and arrogant say, "I know that" and move along.

②

People who are confident and positive ask themselves, "How good am I at that?" and seek to improve.

— Jeffrey Gitomer

Reading is fundamental to attitude self-awareness

You can start by reading and studying these four books:

1. *Think and Grow Rich*
   by Napoleon Hill

2. *How to Win Friends & Influence People*
   by Dale Carnegie

3. *How to Stop Worrying and Start Living*
   by Dale Carnegie

4. *The Power of Positive Thinking*
   by Norman Vincent Peale

Me? I read two pages from a positive book every day. I've been doing 15 minutes a day of "attitude reading" for 30 years. I don't know if it's working yet. I'll do it for another 35 years, and then that's it – I'm going to quit.

I also recommend that you enroll in the nearest Dale Carnegie program. Carnegie courses are timeless and provide a great attitude foundation.

But I know you. You want more attitude gems *now*, and you want them *free*.

OK, here are 20.5 attitude gems (mental snacks to chew on and digest) I've picked up along the way that I recommend you read, cut out, copy, share with others, post on your wall, and study in a way that you can implement them into your "thought and expression" process:

1. Change your input to change your attitude. If you seek a positive mind and a positive attitude, you MUST expose yourself to positive information and hang around positive people. If you want to achieve positive, you have to surround yourself with it and live it.

2. You were born to win. But, "You must plan to win, prepare to win, and expect to win." (A famous Zig Ziglar quote.)

3. "The will to win is nothing without the will to prepare to win." (A [famous coach] Vince Lombardi quote.)

4. You will get whatever you want if you help enough people get whatever they want. A quote that many claim to have said. It doesn't matter who said it – just live it.

5. Make every day as productive as the day before you go on vacation. That's a day that EVERYTHING gets done.

6. Ignore people who tell you, "You can't." (Except your boss.) People will try to discourage you for fear that you will pass them. Don't let it happen.

7. "If you have nothing nice to say, say nothing." (A famous quote said by your mother.)

8. Don't dwell on (whine about) the problem; concentrate on the solution. Resolve how you can; don't lament why you can't.

9. Forgive and go forward. Grudge blocks positive. Until you clear the past, you are destined to repeat it.

10. Self-talk equals self-performance. Look at any athlete. Self-talk is a crucial part of expected positive performance.

11. What is the picture you have of yourself? That is what you will become. Spend 15 minutes a day focusing on a positive picture.

12. You will hear the word "No" 116,000 times in your lifetime. (Maybe more.) Try converting just 1,000 of them to "*YES!*" and the world is your oyster.

13. What you do off the job determines what you are likely to do on the job. Uh oh.

14. Strengthen your weaknesses and strengthen your strengths at the same time. Combine positive with negative for better personal development results.

15. Failure is an event, not a person. Think of failure as "it," not "me."

16. It's not what happens to you; it's what you do with what happens to you. Sound familiar? Attitude manifests itself in your RESPONSE to events.

17. Every obstacle presents an opportunity, if you're looking for it. "Revel" and "lament" are choices. Your choices.

18. Hard work makes luck. Nothing affects positive circumstance and results more than hard work.

19. How many of your problems are cured with ten grand? (A question a famous father [my dad] once asked me as I lamented my problems.) If money makes your problems go away, attitude can make them go away as well.

20. It's not what you say; it's how you say it. The tone of your verbiage determines the atmosphere of your environment.

20.5 Resign your position as general manager of the universe. (A famous author's [me!] principle 12.5 from *The Little Red Book of Selling*.) Don't try to solve (butt into) other people's problems until YOU are problem free.

Attitude gems lead to attitude **AHA!**s – those single moments in time where something happens, or someone says something, and suddenly you get it – suddenly you scream **AHA!** Many (many) years ago, I was driving down the road listening to a tape by Earl Nightingale (one of the founding fathers of personal development). On tape four of his legendary but hard to find series *Direct Line*, the topic was enthusiasm.

"Enthusiasm," Earl said, "comes from the Greek 'entheos,' meaning the God within."

AHA! All of a sudden, all the other quotes and advice made sense. *The strength of self-belief is within your own spirit, if you hunger for the feeling.* And these words are food for yours.

What determines effective communication?

Your Ability to Listen...	**30%**
Your Ability to Respond...	**20%**
Your Attitude...	**50%**

What determines effective customer service?

Your Ability to Listen...	**30%**
Your Ability to Respond...	**20%**
Your Attitude...	**50%**

Half of your *success*
is determined by your
positive attitude.

The plot thickens...

Several national tests have revealed the following startling statistics about why people fail on the job:

20% Improper training. Poor job skills.

15% Poor verbal and written communication skills.

15% Poor or problematic boss or management.

50% Attitude.

Sounds almost impossible, doesn't it?

People can succeed 50% more if they just change the way they think. Earl Nightingale reveals the secret of a positive attitude in his legendary and easy-to-find recording, *The Strangest Secret*:

"You become what you think about..."

But, it's a dedicated discipline that must be practiced, **EVERY DAY!**

You can have a 50% better chance for success, at anything you do, if you start with the simple understanding that:

Quality performance starts with a positive attitude!

– Jeffrey Gitomer

In business, how is attitude related to hunger?

Poor attitude leads to poor communication.

Poor communication leads to poor service.

Poor service leads to no customers.

No customers leads to no company.

No company leads to no job.

No job leads to no money.

No money leads to no food.

If you're craving better food – more filet mignon and fewer hamburgers – the simple rules are: The better your attitude, the better you'll eat. The better your attitude, the more you'll succeed. The better your attitude, the better you'll feel when your day is done.

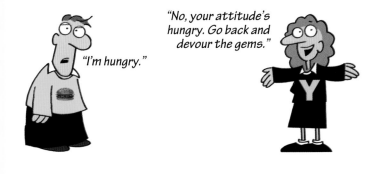

"No, your attitude's hungry. Go back and devour the gems."

"I'm hungry."

In business, here's how your attitude is related to your success

Positive thought leads to positive attitude.

Positive attitude leads to *YES!*Attitude.

*YES!*Attitude leads to *YES!* communication.

YES! communication leads to great customer service.

Great customer service leads to loyal customers.

Loyal customers leads to a successful business.

A successful business leads to a profitable business.

A profitable business leads to your paycheck.

Your paycheck leads to your lifestyle.

It's a combination of your attitude, your achievement at work, and your lifestyle that create your success. The interesting part about success is that everyone defines it in their own terms. The reason attitude plays such a major role is because *you* decide when you have become successful, not others.

In business, your positive thoughts and lifestyle choices lead to your personal success and your career success.

– Jeffrey Gitomer

Missing two footers?

In 1960, at age 14, I met a college basketball coach on the court and asked him for his best, niftiest pointer. He took the ball, walked under the basket, and shot an easy layup.

"See that shot?" he said gruffly. "Ninety-nine percent of all basketball games are won with that shot. Don't miss it." And he walked away. I felt cheated that day, but 20 years later, I realized it was the best business lesson I ever got.

Concentrate on the fundamentals. Ninety-nine percent of all success is achieved that way.

The science of serving and selling in business has nothing to do with nuclear physics or brain surgery.

It's about asking questions, helping others, and believing in yourself, your product, and your company. It's about establishing long-term relationships and having fun. It's all fundamentals.

You don't need to be a professional ballplayer. You just need to know how to shoot layups and *not miss them*.

I received a fax from a guy named Richard Thompson. He said, "Thanks for the article on basics and attitude. My son's basketball team lost last night by missing two footers. I'm sure I have lost sales and customers by missing easy, basic shots."

GET REAL WITH YOUR ATTITUDE:

- **How many games (service and sales opportunities) are you losing because you have the attitude of a loser?**

- **How are you serving others in a friendly, positive way to create a winning atmosphere for your company, your customers, and especially YOU?**

- **How many two footers are you missing because you're not concentrating on the fundamentals of the game?**

There is less than two feet between yes and no. Close the gap.

Free GitBit: **Want to know the fundamental rules of attitude?** Go to www.gitomer.com, register if you are a first-time user, and enter the word FUNDAMENTALS in the GitBit box.

"If you think you can... or if you think you can't... you're right."

– Henry Ford

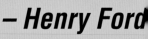

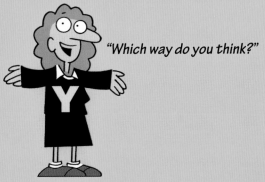

"Which way do you think?"

Think again

Think about your attitude and think about what affects it. Do you know what can influence it one way or the other? For most people, it's always the little things.

Think about the things that negatively influence you, the things that can bust your positive attitude. Ninety-nine percent (or higher) of these things fall into the category of "no big deal." The only problem is, when they happen – at that moment – they seem like a big deal.

My hope is that by making you aware that these little things bust your attitude, subconsciously you'll begin to get over them before they happen again.

*"Can you vaccinate me against negativity?
Everybody I work with seems to have the disease,
and I'm afraid I'll catch it."*

How do negative thoughts and feelings affect you?

- They drain your energy.

- They BLOCK positive thought.

- They cause stress.

- They cause worry.

- They cause illness.

- They BLOCK creative thought.

- They cause errors.

- They reduce productivity.

- They cause anger.

- They prolong painful situations.

- They affect the way you listen to others.

- They affect the way you communicate with others.

- They affect the way you deal with others.

- They take the fun out of your life.

What makes attitude go (stay) bad?

Here are 10.5 attitude busters:

1. Someone has done me wrong.
2. I need more money than I have.
3. Outside influences are affecting me.
4. Outside pressures are affecting me.
5. I have bad luck.
6. I don't like where I live.
7. I don't like my spouse.
8. I don't like my boss.
9. I don't like my co-workers.
10. I don't like my job.
10.5 I don't like myself.

Attitude busters occur because you let them. Things happen, and people interact with you, and your reaction determines if they "get" to your attitude.

KEEP READING: Some real "head nodders" are about to follow. They are the things or people who can get to your attitude – if you let them.

Real-world attitude busters

Minor car accident.

The flu.

A sick child.

Bad day at work.

Lousy service.

Not getting your way.

Having to visit someone you don't want to visit.

In general, being grouchy.

In general, being cynical.

In general, seeing things from why it didn't happen rather than why it could have happened.

Not feeling liked.

Waiting in a long line.

Losing something.

Being jilted.

Hanging around people you don't like.

Discovering a dent in your car.

Having something stolen from you.

Getting a speeding ticket.

The weather.

Having to do something you don't want to do.

Traffic.

Your team losing.

Other people being late.

Being overweight.

Feeling unattractive.

Not being served the right food in a restaurant.

Not feeling liked.

Not fitting in.

Guilt.

Being made to do something you don't really want to do.

Attitude busters have two elements: things and people

Shit happens. And people happen. Or shit people happen. They will either bust you (and your positive attitude) or build you based on the way you react to them.

Unfortunately, the knee-jerk reaction is negative.

THE SECRET TO KEEPING YOUR POSITIVE ATTITUDE: (while others try to bust it) Is hesitation, thought, and questioning before making a statement.

Your reaction to the negative crap, or the negative people who enter your life, is the fate of your attitude.

If your instinct is negative, you can reverse it by reversing your thoughts and actions.

Once you realize that most negative energy comes from outside, it's easier to deal with it.

Positive things and *YES!* things that BUST attitude busters

2

Looking at "material" things as "replaceable" things.

Anything funny.

Personal meditation.

Taking a walk.

Personal positive self-talk.

Helping others without expectation.

Random acts of kindness.

Small daily success.

Persist to small achievement.

Hanging around successful people.

Anything inspirational.

Anything motivational.

Killing people with kindness.

Most things educational.

Something that you do with passion.

Talking to a child.

It ain't the rain, the snow, the boss, the competition, the spouse, the money, the car, the job, or the kids – it's you! And it always has been.

2

– Jeffrey Gitomer

The 3.5 attitude awareness elements that lead you to action

2

1. ATTITUDE AWARENESS OF YOURSELF.

Be selfish. Get your own attitude first. "Secure your own mask first, before helping others." Same with attitude.

Be selfish. Do it for yourself. You have to be selfish in a positive way not selfish in a negative way. You can't say, "It's my ball. I'm taking my ball and going home." That's negative selfish.

POSITIVE SELFISH IS: I'm doing this for someone else because it makes me feel good.

POSITIVE SELFISH IS: I'm wanting to help others because it makes me feel good.

POSITIVE SELFISH IS: I'm reading this book alone because it makes me think better.

POSITIVE SELFISH IS: I'm reading this book because it makes me feel better, or act better.

POSITIVE SELFISH IS: I want to build the best attitude I can for myself, so that I can be the best person I can be for others.

2. ATTITUDE AWARENESS OF OTHERS.

What's your attitude when you describe a person?

When someone asks you, "What do you think about Bill?" do you give your opinion in negative terms – what Bill can't do – or where Bill falls short?

On rare occasions, you might have nice things to say at the beginning, followed by the word BUT. And *but* is the downside. "He's a great guy, *but* he drinks too much."

People put others down to build themselves up. This is known as limited self-image through the third person. "I believe I'm better than Bill; therefore, I can put Bill down."

KEY AWARENESS: You've been doing it for years – so many years that you do it automatically. I'm going to ask you to think about how you describe others in their absence versus how you might describe them if they were in your presence. One usually gives negative traits in their absence, but would almost never say the same thing in their presence. My rule is real simple: If you wouldn't say it to their face, why would you say it behind their back?

This is a very important part of attitude awareness because it brings to focus how much negativity and how much negative talk is really in your life. This is only one example.

> "If you have nothing nice to say about someone, say nothing."
>
> – Florence Gitomer
> 1915-1986 (my mother)

3. ATTITUDE AWARENESS OF THINGS.

What's your attitude when you describe situations or things?

Take a look at all the "things" you have acquired over the years. How many of them have brought you long-term happiness? Oh sure, many of them brought you temporary happiness, even temporary euphoria, but long-term happiness doesn't come from things. It comes from attitude.

If your focus is on things, and the acquisition of things, your drive to acquire them will often be in spite of the good things you should be acquiring on the inside. People who concentrate on the acquisition of material things take shortcuts to acquire them and skip the steps necessary to build long-term attitude in exchange for short-term self-gratification.

The Internet has added to this mess, because you can acquire anything in an instant. You no longer have to go to the store for gratification. You can just click and buy. Don't you wish you could just click and learn? Click and have a better attitude? Click and be successful? Click and be fulfilled?

REALITY CLICK: It's possible. Understand that if you study every day instead of concentrating on material things, one day your attitude will just click. And all the things you're hoping to acquire will just show up.

3.5 BEWARE AND BE AWARE.

Your attitude will be tested every day.

LIFE HAPPENS: Throughout the course of living life, illness, bad breaks, fender benders, traffic, bad weather, rejection, something not going your way, lost game, lost money, arguments, and general frustrations can bring you down. At an unexpected moment's notice.

Anybody can have a good attitude on a good day. Anybody can have a great attitude on a great day. The determination of your attitude takes place when you can have a good attitude or a great attitude (or a **YES!Attitude**) right after a bad event, during a bad time, or when you perceive you're having a bad day.

When things go wrong, you have to be right.
When things go bad, you have to be good.
When things are negative, you have to be positive.
When life says no, you have to think, **YES!**

Up until now, I have made you aware of the elements of both a positive attitude and a negative attitude. You've taken a test to determine how positive your attitude is, or isn't. You've created your definition of a positive attitude and determined where you are on the attitude scale.

"Now, it's time to take ACTION!"

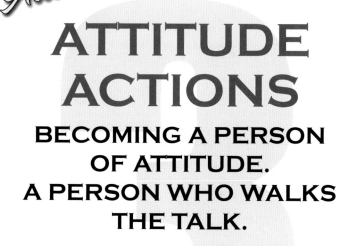

ATTITUDE ACTIONS

BECOMING A PERSON OF ATTITUDE. A PERSON WHO WALKS THE TALK.

Now that you have an understanding of the attributes of attitude, and have a new awareness of what it takes to attain and master those attributes, it's time to take ACTION.

Actions you can take right now

Substitute these for the ones you're presently using:

Be nice.	Praise others.
Be kind.	Take responsibility.
Smile.	Be proud of your work.
Make friends.	
Say nice things.	Be proud of your accomplishments.

Don't worry, be happy.

These are actions that your mother has already told you at least a thousand times. If she's still alive, call her on the phone **right now** and thank her for planting the seeds of positive attitude in your head. Then apologize to her for thinking, at the time she was planting the seeds, that she was nagging you.

I'm sure you have found in your life, the same way I have found in mine, that the older you become, the smarter your parents seem to get. Please thank them now, while you still can.

An attitude-action lesson you can begin to use the minute you read it

Substitute the words "I'm sorry" with the words "Thank you!"

When people yell at you or blame you, don't blame someone else, or say "I'm sorry," or grovel. Just say, "Thank you!"

3

Think about how you feel when someone yells at you. It's not the most pleasant feeling in the world. Most people have an instant reaction to either defend themselves, blame someone else, or apologize profusely. With a **YES!Attitude**, none of these are acceptable.

If you say, "Thank you. I appreciate you bringing this to my attention. Now that I know about it, I can fix it right away," your words clearly state an implied apology, a desire to take action, and a ton of self-confidence. You are expressing your attitude in the form of positive action.

"I'm sorry" is a state of being. If you state it enough, you become it. If you want to make amends, just say, "I apologize." But an apology does not indicate action. "Thank you" indicates acceptance, and the words that follow indicate you're willing to do something about it.

A *YES!* Attitude is the difference between saying "I'm sorry," and saying "Thank you!"

3

– Jeffrey Gitomer

An alternative to this "Thank you" action is asking a question. But the question still begins with thank you. For example, say, "Thank you for bringing this to my attention. I was wondering if you could tell me how this came about so that I can figure out the best immediate solution?"

With this strategy, you make the person think about what happened and begin to create meaningful dialogue.

Either way, the words "Thank you" have overpowered the words "I'm sorry." And either way, you've turned a negative to a positive in under three seconds. The cool part about this lesson is that you can even teach it to your children.

It's incredible!

When you substitute the words "Thank you" followed by the words "I appreciate" for "I'm sorry," the results will:

- **Amaze you.**
- **Lead you closer to the truth.**
- **Make you a better person.**
- **Gain the respect of others.**

In this book, I have quoted Earl Nightingale and his legendary personal development message from *The Strangest Secret*: "You become what you think about." But what I didn't say is that you also become what you talk about.

ATTITUDE PERCEPTION IS ALL IN THE FIRST FEW WORDS: The way the other person hears your words determines his or her thoughts of you. Your words reflect your attitude. This is where **YES!Attitude** begins to take over.

There are prime starting phrases that will get the ball rolling in the right direction – the **YES!** direction.

After someone makes a request, or asks a question, or gripes – and before you answer the request or question them – you *start* your response with words like:

Great!	**I think I can help!**
No problem!	**YES!**
That's my favorite problem!	**Cool!**
I think we can solve…	**Can do!**
I'm sure there's a way…	**Consider it done!**

HINT: Say these responses the way you would want to hear them. You can also ask a question. Anything instead of making a negative statement.

Want to start making an attitude change? Take attitude actions

Think negative or think positive – it's a choice and a process. Negative is (unfortunately) an instinctive process. Positive thinking is a learned self-discipline that must be studied and practiced every day.

To achieve a positive attitude, you must take physical, verbal, and mental **ACTIONS**.

Here are 15.5 chunks of attitude awareness and actions to help put you (and keep you) on the positive path:

1. Admit it's no one's fault but yours. The more you blame others, the less chance you have to think positive thoughts, see a positive solution, and take positive action toward a solution. The opposite of blame is responsibility. Your first responsibility is to control your inner thoughts and thought directions.

2. Understand you always have (had) a choice. Attitude is a choice, and most people select from the negative column. Reason? It's more natural to blame and defend than it is to admit and take responsibility.

3. If you think it's okay, it is. If you think it's not okay, it's not. Your thoughts direct your attitude to a path. If you think, "This is crappy. Why does this always happen to me?" you have chosen a path. If you think "WOW! This may not be the greatest, but look what I'm learning," you've chosen the **YES!** path.

4. Invest your time, don't spend it. Ignore the local junk news. Find a project, or make a plan to sell something or meet with someone who can buy what you're selling instead. Spend (invest) an hour a day in anything, and in five years, you will become a world-class expert. The only question is: At what? Most people will become a world-class expert at some kind of local TV news program or some kind of TV rerun. Me? I read and write while you watch TV. **REMEMBER:** News = Negative. Books or CDs = Positive.

5. Study the thoughts and writings of positive people. Read Napoleon Hill's *Think and Grown Rich*. TWICE. Then, get Norman Vincent Peale's audio series *The Power of Positive Thinking*. His words are priceless, timeless gems of wisdom that you can convert to your own success thoughts. Listen to CDs by the positive thinkers of the world: Zig Ziglar, Dennis Waitley, Wayne Dyer, and as many others as you can find. The secret is to listen to a little each day.

6. Attend seminars and take courses on attitude. Start at the top. Enroll in a Dale Carnegie program. The hardest part of taking an attitude course is finding one. Look at any school or university in the world and try to find one course on attitude in any of them. I'll save you the time – there aren't any.

7. Check your language gauge. Do you say "half full" or "half empty"? "Partly cloudy" or "partly sunny"? They're just words, but they are a reflection of how your mind sees things and an indication of how you process thoughts.

8. Avoid confrontational and negative words. The worst ones are why, can't, and won't. A loaf of bread has two beginnings – not two ends.

9. Say why you LIKE things and people, not why you don't. I like my job because… I like his attitude because… I love my family because… Say things from the positive side enough, and it will become a habit you will revel in for life.

10. Help others without expectation or measuring. If you think someone "owes you one," you are counting or measuring. If you give help away freely, you don't ever have to worry about the measurement. The world will reward you ten times over.

11. Think about your winning and losing words. Be aware of "loser" phrases and expressions. Lose with, "They don't pay me enough to…" or "That's not my job." If you say, "I'm not 'cause he's not," who loses? If you say, "Why should I when he…," who loses? Think "learn," "lessons," "experience," and "solutions" before you make a statement.

12. Think about your mood and your mood swings. How long do you stay in a bad mood? If it's more than five minutes, something's wrong. And over time, your attitude (and your relationships, and your results, and your success) will suffer.

13. Are you the head of the complaint department AND the chief complainer? Many people slip into a cynicism day by day. They become bitter because of their jealousy or envy of other people or their own misfortune. BIG MISTAKE. List the lessons you can learn from those you have bitterness for, and the results will turn your thinking toward your own success – and away from theirs.

14. Celebrate victory AND defeat. In my early days of selling, I would go to a department store and buy myself something every time I made a sale. It made me feel GREAT! When someone told me to celebrate victory AND defeat, I started to buy myself something after I lost a sale, too. Felt GREAT. After a while, I was feeling GREAT all the time. Winning and losing are part of life and apart from attitude.

15. Visit a children's hospital or help someone less fortunate than you. Get comfortable with the plight of others, and feel good about the minuteness of your problems compared to theirs.

15.5 Count your blessings every day. Make the list as long as you can. If you are fortunate enough to have it, start with health. Add the love of children and family. From there, it's easy to build the list.

Want an instant lesson? Go out and buy a copy of Watty Piper's *The Little Engine That Could*. Or, go to your kid's room and get the copy full of crayon marks. Read it regularly. It's not just a book for kids; it's a philosophy for a lifetime.

What does the local news have to do with success? Nothing!

Watching the local news – there's a great use of your time. Thirty to sixty minutes a day of useless information, presented in one-hundred-percent problem format.

"If it bleeds, it leads." That's the local news philosophy of presenting information. How does that affect your success? In the worst ways possible.

No one watching the news cares that your sales numbers are up, or that Frank got a promotion, or that Billy got all A's on his report card. Good news doesn't sell; therefore, it's omitted.

Rather, what you get is distorted, negative information about two to three percent of the people affecting those who view it in the worst way possible.

NOTE WELL: I am **NOT** saying don't watch (or read) business news. Information that can impact your industry, or your customer, should be watched and read intently.

What does watching the local news have to do with being of service? Negative nothing. Serving is *solution* based; the local news is *problem* based.

If you watch an hour a day of problems, every day for years, you become problem-oriented. Then, you drag the news crap to work and begin to negatively affect others with your pukey stories. *Hey, did you hear what happened on the news…?* (Barf!) The news sickness is contagious. You get it by watching and then infect others by telling them about it.

Do you think local news adds or detracts from your serving skills? How about your business skills? How about your life skills? How about your selling skills?

"Hey, Jeffrey," you say, "the news is the most popular show on television." It's popular because most of the people watching it lack direction or focus, or are miserable and looking for something or someone more miserable than they are – I guess to make them feel better.

Need to know the weather? Poke your head outside in the morning. It's a lot more accurate than the weather guy.

Think the local news is so important? Got to watch it every day to keep up? What happened last Tuesday? What happened yesterday? Same crap, different day.

Think the local news is worthy of your time? How many of you can look in the mirror and say, "I'm successful today. I'm where I am today, because I watched the local news."

See what I mean? By the way, the same goes for any television rerun. (But not Seinfeld. Seinfeld is funny.)

HERE'S A WAKE-UP CALL: (If you're still not convinced.)
Let's say you've been watching the news a half hour a day
for the past year. That's 7.5 full 24-hour days you spent
watching problems. In five years, that's 38 full 24-hour days.
In terms of a 40-hour workweek, that's 23 weeks every five
years – and that's only if you watch the 6 o'clock news. If
you tune in for more crap at 11 o'clock, double it! That's the
equivalent of 46, 40-hour workweeks.

Imagine the possibilities if you diverted that energy in a
positive direction. Imagine what you could do with that
time, and accomplish in that time, if you put it to productive
use for yourself. WOW! (By the way, you don't want to
know the 20-year figure – it's too scary).

Which do you think is a more powerful use of your time: watching other people's problems or investing in yourself and creating plans and solutions?

Here are four solution-based uses of your time:

Read. Trade journals, self-help books, positive attitude
books, anything humorous, sales books, trendsetting
books, and annual reports and brochures of your biggest
customers. Study.

Listen. Self-help CDs. Nightingale Conant (Chicago) has a catalog of thousands of hours of profound, impactful information. *Invest.*

Mastermind. Attract (smart) friends and associates to your house once a week to create new ideas and action plans. *Invite.*

Compute. This includes writing, planning, learning, and Internetting. The computer is the biggest link to the twenty-first century. Master it. *Explore.*

The next time you say, "I don't have enough time," substitute that phrase with, "I don't choose to spend my time in that manner." It's closer to the truth. The *real* truth is that you're not investing your time in the most important person in the world – **you!**

As I said before, if you devote the time you currently spend watching TV to learning, you could be an international expert on *anything.*

Me? I studied sales and wrote about sales, instead of watching the news.

After two and a half years, I published my first book, *The Sales Bible.* In those two and a half years, which do you think helped my career more: watching the news, or reading and writing for an hour each morning?

What are you doing with your hour?

It's about time!

Take your hour a day and convert it into positive action or learning – for yourself, your job, your business, and your family.

At the end of one year, you will have captured more than 15 full 24-hour days for building your future. **YES***!*

"The news depresses me, so I print my own newspaper. It's called I'm The Greatest. Every page has positive stuff about ME!"

Watch your world change

Try this *YES!*Attitude action:

Pick something you love, and do it an hour a day for a year.

Try this *YES!*Attitude action:

Move the TV remote to a remote location, and begin reading about (and for the benefit of) the most important person in the world – you.

Try this *YES!*Attitude action:

Set your alarm clock 30 minutes earlier than you have it set right now. Jump out of bed, clear your head, and go to your personal "alone space." Read from a positive book, or write positive thoughts and actions.

The daily dose of attitude

It's real simple.

> You wake up in the morning
> and you read something positive,
> or something inspirational, or
> something educational. Then you
> write your thoughts and ideas.

***YES!* ACTION 1:** Talk about what you learned.

***YES!* ACTION 2:** Act on what you learned.

***YES!* ACTION 3:** Start your day with a great attitude.

Is that simple or what? All you have to do is do that every day for one year, and I promise you'll have the habit forever.

Free Git✗Bit: **Do you have an attitude library?** If not, go to www.gitomer.com, register if you are a first-time user, and enter the words ATTITUDE LIBRARY in the GitBit box. I will honor your privacy, and the information is free.

The list of books you will get contains my recommendations for books to **BUY** for *your* library. Don't go to the library like a cheap bastard. **BUY THE BOOKS**. Attitude books are not just for the reading. They're meant to be reread and used forever as a reference.

How can I be more positive with my children?

ATTITUDE ACTIONS WHEN YOUR KIDS DO SOMETHING WRONG:

1. Never yell at them.
2. Instead, ask what they did.
3. Then *ask* if this was the BEST they could have done.
4. Ask them what could have been done differently.
5. Ask them if they think they can do that the next time.
5.5 Encourage them to do right after they've done wrong.

LIFELONG ATTITUDE ACTIONS:

1. Get them to love school at an early age.
2. Fight to get them good teachers.
3. Do homework WITH them.
4. Never put them down.
4.5 Speak to them with a *YES!*Attitude.

How can I be more positive with my spouse?

ATTITUDE ACTIONS:

1. Be a partner, not a spouse.
2. Surprise her – surprise him.
3. Compliment at all times.
4. Stay humorous, but never make fun of.
5. Stay affectionate.
5.5 Be interested in each other and each other's interests.

How can I be more positive at home?

ATTITUDE ACTIONS:

1. Praise others.
2. Don't belittle.
3. If "familiarity breeds contempt" lives at your house, kill it.
3.5 You know the buttons. Don't push them.

NOTE: Home attitude determines work attitude.

How can I be more positive at work?

ATTITUDE ACTIONS:

1. Put a "quote of the day" on everyone's desk.

2. Use positive language.

3. Be willing to do for others without measuring.

4. Be willing to help others without measuring.

5. Be an example for others to follow.

6. Ask one more question before you answer.

7. Don't join the bashing.

8. Don't join the pity party.

9. Don't join the revolt.

10. Solve, rather than complain.

11. Get the third party being talked about negatively into the conversation.

12. Quit whining.

12.5 Start with *YES!*

Bust the attitude busters
10.5 attitude buster REMEDIES

On page 73, I gave you a list of attitude busters, things to be aware of.

Here are the busters again, with actions (remedies) you can take to overcome them:

1. Someone has done me wrong. Do your best to make it right, and then forgive them. No vengeance. Ever.

2. I need more money than I have. Make more sales.

3. Outside influences are affecting me. This requires concentration and a change of scenery. Get away from the influencers and the influences. If you don't, you'll go down.

4. Outside pressures are affecting me. Don't give in, even if your ass falls off. Get to safe ground and stay there.

5. I have bad luck. Hard work makes luck.

6. I don't like where I live. Move.

7. I don't like my spouse. Make peace. Remember why you got married in the first place. Renew vows. Or if all else fails, get a new one.

8. I don't like my boss. Get a new one.

9. I don't like my co-workers. Get a new job. **NOTE:** If you don't like all of them, the problem may be you.

10. I don't like my job. Get a new one. Do something you LOVE. Life's too short to do anything else.

10.5 I don't like myself. List your best qualities. You'll be surprised how much there is to love.

I have just given you "tip-of-the-iceberg" answers (actions). There are many more. Why not take some personal time, get introspective, and discover what they really are for you?

"You're waiting for a positive mood to come in and take over? Should I unlock the front door?"

Wanna start on YOUR path to positive attitude?

Sure you do!

Take these 2.5 immediate actions:

1. Focus in. Concentrate on yourself. Follow attitude gem 20.5 on page 61 and resign your position as general manager of the universe. You can't be involved in other people's problems until your own are gone. And when you're building your own attitude, you *must* take the time (even though it seems selfish) to be the *best* you can be for yourself *first*. This single step will also pave the way for you to be the best you can be for others.

2. Work at it a small amount each day. The daily dose of "attitude adjustment" is the most important part of the positive attitude achievement process. An apple a day. Not 7 apples on Sunday or 31 apples at the end of the month.

2.5 You gotta do them EVERY DAY for the next 25 years. The one thing you cannot do is take your attitude for granted. If you've played sports, you know that practice is a critical part of your ability to play well – especially if you're a professional athlete. Attitude is exactly the same. It requires daily practice to keep your physical skills and your mental skills sharp.

Wanna continue on the path to *YES!*Attitude?

The secret to gaining your *YES!*Attitude is…

Start with *YES!*

Start all conversations with what can be done.

Attitude has a language of *YES!* or NO!
Convert "no" language to "*YES!*" language.

Tell me what you can do, not what you can't. Tell me the solution, don't puke on me.

MY PERSONAL ATTITUDE LESSON: My father, Max, always made me come to him with the solution whenever I had a "problem." Sometimes, I was granted permission, but most times he said, "Got it all figured out, son?" That meant *dumb idea.* But he made me think "solution."

I miss my dad. If yours is still alive, call him and ask for some advice. Do it often.

3.5 principles that lead to success, wealth, and *YES!* Attitude

Many people get into a career to "make money." There could not be a worse reason to enter a profession. The best way to amass a lot of money in a career is to earn it.

NOTE WELL: I didn't say *make* money, I said *earn* money. In serving others, you don't make money – you earn it. The biggest reason people fail is the philosophy, "I'm in this to make money," or "I'm in this because it's where the money is."

Everyone wants to earn a million dollars for different reasons. But you all need (want) money to achieve your goals and dreams. How do you get the money? By living and executing the 3.5 principles of wealth building.

1. You earn money by building a strong self-belief system.

2. You earn money by being better than the rest.

3. You earn money by having answers that others don't.

3.5 You earn money by loving what you do and having a *YES!* Attitude about life.

Here's a brief overview of each principle:

Building belief is…Having the confidence that you can do whatever you set your mind to do. Knowing *why* you want to earn a fortune and living the dream by having the confidence to take action. How are you building that belief now?

Being better than the rest is…Having the attitude to do whatever it takes to excel at what you do. Getting up one hour earlier. Striving to be the best at everything. And not being willing to settle for second place. There is no prize for second place in job promotions.

Learning new answers is…Having the attitude to expose yourself to success information that you don't now have, but need, to be the best. Seminars, books, CDs – a plan of lifelong learning. There is only one way to get answers. *By learning them.* It seems simple – just not easy. Some people have to go through failure to get them. Some have a steady diet of exposing themselves to new information every day. If you want to build wealth, build a wealth of knowledge. The key is *learning something new every day.*

How are you getting those answers now? Have you put yourself in a position to get the knowledge you need – to earn the money you want to achieve your dreams?

"The biggest reason people don't succeed is that they don't expose themselves to existing information," says the GREAT Jim Rohn. And I add to that, *People don't have the attitude of learning because they don't love what they do enough to want to be the BEST at it.*

It's not so important that you want to succeed; it's critical you know *why* you want to succeed and what has prevented you from achieving your success to date. What **belief system** and **game plan** do you need to put in place to gain that success?

WARNING: If you read the last paragraph and blamed everyone and everything but yourself, you are doomed. Take responsibility for the failure, and do something about it. (I'll guarantee when you succeed, you'll take the responsibility.)

It's easy to lose self-belief if the one you've got in place is weak due to poor knowledge, lack of determination, and lack of love of what you do. It's easy to fail at your job if you have never told yourself (sold yourself) the real reason you want success in the first place. Not earning money for money's sake, but *the real reason you want the money,* and *what you'll do with it once you get it.*

For example, you may want money for a specific college that you want your child to attend. Or it may be to liberate you from a spouse or to say "I DID IT!" to a sibling or a parent. Whatever it is, uncover it, write it down, post it up (if possible), carry it with you, and read it twice a day. Then you will begin to live it.

Combine your "why" with the desire and dedication to be the best and a passion for what you do, and presto, career success!

Some of you are
reading this and saying,
"Jeffrey, don't bug me with
this philosophy stuff.
Tell me how to
make more money."

I am.

3

Self-belief is the most powerful attitude lesson I can deliver.

Only a few will get it.
The ones who will
rise to *YES!*

Building belief.
Your belief...

Everyone has a reason *why*. Some have many. Why they have chosen their path. Why they believe in what they do. Why they want to succeed. Why they want to help others. Why they want to be the best.

I'm convinced that uncovering your personal "why" (which may be deeper than you think) and strengthening that belief system will lead you to be the **BEST** person you can be.

WHY AM I IN MY PRESENT JOB?

_____

_____

_____

WHY DO I BELIEVE IN MYSELF?

_____

_____

_____

WHY DO I BELIEVE IN MY COMPANY?

_____

_____

_____

WHY DO I WANT TO IMPROVE MY CAREER AND JOB SKILLS?

_____

_____

_____

WHY DO I BELIEVE IN MY ABILITY TO HELP OTHER PEOPLE?

_____

_____

_____

WHY DO I WANT TO BE THE BEST AT WHAT I DO?

_____

_____

_____

What do I need to do to build a stronger belief system…

IN MY PROFESSION?

_____

_____

_____

IN MY COMPANY?

_____

_____

_____

IN MYSELF?

_____

_____

_____

The shortest goal lesson of your life

FINAL ATTITUDE ACTION: Post your goals (in front of your face) on your bathroom mirror, and say them twice a day. Once achieved, post your accomplishments on your bedroom mirror so you can start each day by looking at your success.

SECRET: Looking at your past successes reinforces your ability to achieve your present goals.

3

"I think I should add, GET A BETTER RAZOR."

YES! Attitude

ATTITUDE ATTRIBUTES

Unsolicited e-mail I received after delivering a seminar:
"I love your positive thinking.
I love the way your
thoughts are always so positive.
It makes me want to
hang around you."

Unsolicited question for you:
Who wants to hang around you?

Think about your BEST qualities

Think about the things that you love to do. Think about the things that you consider yourself damn good at. Think about the qualities that other people compliment you on.

Maybe it's the way you speak. Maybe it's the way you treat other people. Maybe it's the way you volunteer in the community. Maybe it's the way you dress. Maybe it's the way you conduct your business.

Those qualities make you the person that you are.

They're not just your BEST qualities. They're your attributes, your assets. The same holds true for attitude.

If you have the right qualities, if you have the right attributes, if you have the right attitude assets, then – and only, then – can you achieve a *YES!*Attitude.

The following two pages contain a self-evaluation where I ask you to rate your *YES!*Attitude attributes. I promise that many of them will cause you to think before you answer. And I promise that they will create a new sense of awareness and action on your part, in order for you to build a solid foundation for your lifelong *YES!*Attitude.

Rate your
YES! Attitude attributes.
A self-evaluation

HERE'S HOW: Circle a number for each attribute that is closest to your present situation. At the end of the test, calculate your total score by adding up all the numbers you circled.

1=Never 2=Rarely 3=Sometimes 4=Frequently 5=All the time

❑	I wake up happy.	1 2 3 4 5
❑	I think **YES!** first.	1 2 3 4 5
❑	I smile.	1 2 3 4 5
❑	I am kind to others.	1 2 3 4 5
❑	I have deep self-belief.	1 2 3 4 5
❑	I am self-confident.	1 2 3 4 5
❑	I take responsibility for my actions.	1 2 3 4 5
❑	I motivate and inspire myself.	1 2 3 4 5
❑	I affirm myself.	1 2 3 4 5
❑	I have great spirit.	1 2 3 4 5
❑	I think positive at work and at home.	1 2 3 4 5
❑	I laugh a lot.	1 2 3 4 5
❑	I find humor in all things.	1 2 3 4 5
❑	I read positive things.	1 2 3 4 5

┐ I'm in a consistent "good mood."   **1 2 3 4 5**

┐ I desire to be the **BEST**.   **1 2 3 4 5**

┐ I love what I do.   **1 2 3 4 5**

┐ I am happy on the inside.   **1 2 3 4 5**

┐ I encourage and compliment others.   **1 2 3 4 5**

┐ I look for the good in every situation.   **1 2 3 4 5**

┐ People like me.   **1 2 3 4 5**

┐ People are attracted to me.   **1 2 3 4 5**

TOTAL SCORE _____

Your *YES!*Attitude
attributes report card:

90-110. Your attitude attributes will put you on the path to achievement.

75-89. Your attitude attributes need work, but you're on the right path. Stay on the path, the self-improvement path.

60-74. Your attitude attributes are good, not great. You're headed toward the right path. Dedicate more time to your personal excellence.

Below 60. Somewhere along the line, you've taken the wrong fork in the road. Get back on the path to positive.

4

YES!

HERE'S HOW TO IMPROVE YOUR ATTITUDE WEAKNESSES: Go back to the test and check the box on the left next to any attribute where you rated yourself a 1, 2, or 3.

ONE WEAK A WEEK:

1. Select one weakness each week.

2. Write down your present situation in relation to that attribute.

3. Write down what you could be doing differently to improve.

4. Ask yourself, "What can I do to implement what I know I should be doing, but I'm not?"

5. Decide what action(s) you need to take to improve.

6. Figure out how much time you need to allocate to it.

6.5 Take action until you become the master of each attribute.

NOTE: Don't go too fast. Work on it until you begin to see real improvement. Each attribute is critical to a *YES!*Attitude

A word about philosophy and why it's good

What's your philosophy?

If I ask you what you want to become and how you intend to get there, interspersed within the answer will be your philosophy. It's the "how" and "what" of your achievement expectations.

Most people have a philosophy, but it's not clearly defined. Your philosophy is the driving force behind your attitude. It defines what you will do and how you will act to get where you want to go. It's the motive – and the motivation – behind your thoughts.

PHILOSOPHY PAUSE: Take a break from reading and get to your computer. Create a few sentences that define *who you are* or *what you want to become, what you do* and *how you do it.*

Sneak a peek at mine on page 123. That may make developing yours easier to do, and more understandable.

Write yours and make plans to revisit it monthly for a few years. I have been refining mine for 25 years. I'm close, but a few more subtle revisions remain.

DEEP (SIX-FEET-UNDER) THOUGHT: Think of what you would want your children to say about you at your funeral that would define you as a person of character: How you lived your life, who you helped, who you loved, and how you acted as a person. The actions that you take throughout your life are based on your philosophy.

If you want an insightful, intellectual picture, read *Philosophy: Who Needs It* by Ayn Rand. It will give you powerful insight as to philosophy's importance and relevance in your life. Read slowly. Think quickly.

> All that man achieves,
> and all that he fails to achieve
> is a direct result of
> his own thoughts.
>
> – James Allen
> from *As a Man Thinketh*

Free Git Bit: Already snuck ahead to read my philosophy on page 123? **If you have read it and want to know more about it, or you want to use it as a guide to create your own philosophy, I have defined each principle for better understanding.** To find out more, go to www.gitomer.com, register if you are a first-time user, and enter the word PHILOSOPHY in the GitBit box.

The Great Jim Rohn says...

**PHILOSOPHY DRIVES ATTITUDE.
ATTITUDE DRIVES ACTIONS.
ACTIONS DRIVE RESULTS.
RESULTS DRIVE LIFESTYLES.**

**IF YOU DON'T LIKE YOUR LIFESTYLE, LOOK AT YOUR RESULTS.
IF YOU DON'T LIKE YOUR RESULTS, LOOK AT YOUR ACTIONS.
IF YOU DON'T LIKE YOUR ACTIONS, LOOK AT YOUR ATTITUDE.
IF YOU DON'T LIKE YOUR ATTITUDE,
LOOK AT YOUR PHILOSOPHY.**

"If you have a philosophy of service to others, and if you have a positive attitude, then you can BEGIN to become successful and can BEGIN to take success actions."

"Successful people do what unsuccessful people don't (won't) do. Successful people live outside their comfort zone. Successful people hang around money or things that make money. Successful people are consistent (will be here next year). Successful people stay in the fire. Successful people know how to access information. Successful people are always learning."

These are a few of my notes from a Jim Rohn seminar. I've attended a dozen Jim Rohn seminars. Every time I go, I learn something new. If you ever get a chance to see Jim Rohn live, go.

Here's what other philosophers have to say

"When he who hears does not know what he who speaks means, and when he who speaks does not know what he himself means, that is philosophy."

– Voltaire

"Philosophy is the science which considers truth."

– Aristotle

"The essence of philosophy is that a man should so live that his happiness shall depend as little as possible on external things."

– Epictetus

The sales and life philosophy of Jeffrey Gitomer…

I give value first.
I help other people.
I strive to be the *best* at what I love to do.
I establish long-term relationships with everyone.
I have fun.
…And I do that every day.

Jeffrey Gitomer says…

I'm sharing my
personal philosophy
with you because I want you
to see that it does not
contain the word "attitude."
Rather, my philosophy
EXUDES attitude.

Use my philosophy as a model to write yours.

Your environments and your associations

Think about where you work, where you live, and where you hang out. Those are your environments.

Think about the people in your life: Your family, your spouse, your significant other, your kids, your friends, your co-workers, your boss, your customers, and your professional connections. Those are your associations.

Environments and associations do more to shape your daily attitude and your long-term success than any other elements of your life.

MY QUESTIONS AND CHALLENGES TO YOU:
- **Where are you living?**
- **Where are you working?**
- **Who are you associating with that is helping your attitude and your success?**

AND IF THEY'RE NOT THE BEST ENVIRONMENTS OR THE BEST ASSOCIATIONS:
- **How can you change them?**
- **How can you convert them?**
- **How can you restructure them?**
- **How can you influence them?**

If you just understood that by adjusting some of your existing environments and associations your life would take a quantum leap forward, you'd do it in a second. The reason that you don't step is that you're comfortable where you are standing – however crappy that might be.

Step back and look at the big picture of your life. If you want to grow it and make it permanently positive, you will need to assess your surroundings – living, working, and the people you come in contact with.

Rate the positive impact of your people and places. If the ratings are low, it's time to graduate. Go gracefully, go ethically, go with class – but go.

"I'm going to be rich! I've invented a compass that always points to something positive!"

The "three you're crazy" rule. Who does it apply to?

You get a new job, take a commission-only sales position, start a new venture, or get involved with direct sales or a home-based business. You tell one of your friends about it, and they respond, "You're crazy!" Then you tell your best friend who says, "You're crazy!" Then you tell your mom, and *she* says, "You're crazy!" And then you quit. That's the "three you're crazy" rule. Most people can't get past it. Can you?

You took the new position, or went out on your own, or got involved for one or more of these 2.5 reasons:

1. **You really liked it and thought it would be fun to do.**

2. **The opportunity was fantastic, and you thought you could make (earn) money or gain the experience you needed.**

2.5 **You thought it would get you closer to achieving your dreams.**

People who tell you you're crazy are known as "pukers." Their job is to make you feel stupid, inadequate, or incapable of making good judgments. Pukers are people to avoid at all costs.

Here are some warning signals that someone is puking on you:

- **They tell you to get a real job.**
- **They share examples of failure.**
- **They ridicule your judgment.**
- **They make fun of the imagined outcome.**
- **They tell you that you're sure to lose your money and fail miserably.**

In short, they get to your attitude and your self-confidence, and they question your judgment. **WHEW!** What a drag it is to hear that kind of stuff. Why can't they just encourage you? Or support you? Or ask if they can help you succeed? Or just say, "Way to go!" Why are they saying, "You're crazy!" Why do people put you down instead of build you up?

The main reasons others puke on you is because of:

- **Their own limited self-image.**
- **Their own low self-esteem.**
- **A low opinion of you.**
- **A jealousy of you.**
- **An envy of you.**
- **An environmental reaction. (As in, theirs sucks.)**
- **An attitude reaction. (As in, theirs sucks.)**
- **A reaction of ignorance. (As in, they're stupid.)**

4

YES!

REALITY: Their attitude sucks and they're basically cynical. They are incapable of encouragement because they would rather see you as a failure (just like they are).

So, the first thing to think when someone so graciously pukes on you is, "Cool! They ain't me."

Okay, they're pukers. What do you do about it? How do you handle it? What's the first step to "Pepto Bismol-ing" them?

Here's a one-word clue: **LOOK**.

> **LOOK AT THEIR CAR.**
>
> **LOOK AT THEIR CAREER.**
>
> **LOOK AT THEIR ATTITUDE.**
>
> **LOOK AT THEIR SUCCESS.**
>
> **LOOK AT THEIR LIFESTYLE.**
>
> **LOOK AT THEIR HAPPINESS.**

If you wouldn't trade places with them, who's crazy?

But, that's not the remedy. That's just the setup for understanding how to change your perception of the situation.

Here are 5.5 "puke-stoppers:"

1. Your first inclination is to puke back. Don't stoop to their level. Rise above it.

2. Part ways with positive words. Say, "You might be right. I'll keep you posted with my progress. By the way, if it starts to pay off, when do you want me to give you a chance to get involved?"

3. Be cool and lead by example. If you tell people what you're going to do, do it full force.

4. Change your environment. Find places where success is occurring and invest your time there.

5. Change your associations. Hang around successful people. People who inspire and inform you. People who educate and encourage you. Find role models, not road blocks.

5.5 Don't talk about what you're going to do. Just do it. Too many people brag about what they're going to do, instead of what they did. If you're passionate about what you've chosen, then work at it with the same passion. When you begin to succeed, you won't have to tell anyone. They'll all be watching you.

You see, the only remedy to shut pukers up, and make them go away, is your own success. And even after you begin to succeed, beware of eternal pukers.

The sign of eternal pukers is that they'll say (even when you get to success), "It won't last." Pathetic, aren't they? The real remedy is to *do it for yourself*, not for them. They don't matter.

Memorize and repeat the following mantra as you self-actualize your success. It's a phrase I wrote at five o'clock one morning, and it can change your life once you understand the truth of it:

"The main reason people rain on my parade is because they have no parade of their own."

— *Jeffrey Gitomer*

4

What's so funny?
Everything!

How do you react to the events in your life?
How do you respond to the situations that life presents to you?
What is your tone when you speak to others?

How would someone describe your **HUMOR** or your **SENSE OF HUMOR** or your **PROACTIVE SENSE OF HUMOR**?

When you surf on your TV do you stop at funny or violent? Comedy or drama? When you go to the movies, are they funny or scary?

Which do you look for FIRST?

Me? I seek funny in everything. I have no time for other people's drama and even less time for violence.

Think funny first?

What is your first thought?

LAUGHTER IS MEDICINE: I was riding in a limo from the airport in Houston with my assistant, editor, best friend, and secret weapon, Jessica McDougall. She wasn't feeling well, her back was hurting, and she was lying down across the back seat as best she could.

The driver was horrid. Accelerator, brake, accelerator, brake. Jerking down the road. (You know the type – they gun it, and then slam on the brakes. Or they speed up, and then slow down.) To make matters worse, Jessica is prone to car sickness. The driver found open road but had no sense of maintaining constant speed and kept jerking the car, even with no one in front of him. Jessica was not moving.

I was working on my computer. And I typed in big, bold letters so she could see, **"The driver's name is Lurch!"** We howled. And she started feeling better.

4

Laughter is the best medicine. No, laughter is the first medicine.

FUNNY SELF-TEST: What are your first thoughts? What are your first responses? How do you react to ordinary situations? What do you say? Can you think funny? Can you create a smile? Can you elicit one? What about your eight hours at work? Where's your sense of humor there? How does work impact your sense of humor and your sense of funny?

CAUTION ONE: Funny is not to be confused with cynical.
CAUTION TWO: Funny is not to be confused with biting humor.

SEE IF YOU HAVE THE ATTRIBUTE OF "FUNNY": Do you believe you have a *great* sense of humor? Is your first thought funny? Are your first responses humorous? Are you seeking humor in others? Do you laugh easily and often? Do you love to laugh? Are you happy on the inside?

MAJOR CLUE: If your thinking is "happy," your response can be funny. But not if you don't try it. Laughter, humor, and funny are contagious. If you have these attitude attributes, others can catch them and pass them on. That's not only powerful, but it's also enriching the lives of others. No joke.

*"I shook my head no so many times, my boss
replaced me with a bobblehead doll!"*

Lead with a smile

Jessica McDougall has one of the nicest smiles in the world She also has a positive attitude. I wonder if the two are connected? What do you think?

How much do you SMILE?

A simple smile is a powerful atti-tool:

- **It displays "positive" without saying a word.**
- **It shows your warmth.**
- **It shows your internal feelings, externally.**
- **It shows you're happy.**
- **It shows you're open.**
- **It shows you're confident.**
- **And it sets a tone for the first spoken words.**

Think about the power of a smile: Songs have been written about it. Photographers all over the world urge you to smile every time they take your picture. When babies smile, they light up an entire room and make everyone else smile with them. (And adults will act like total idiots trying to get them to smile again.)

Your smile is one of the greatest attributes and assets you can possess – and it's *free*. All you have to do is use it every minute of every day.

I believe that a smile is *the* attribute of a positive attitude, both for yourself and the perception of others.

4

– *Jeffrey Gitomer*

YES! *Attitude*

ATTITUDE ACHIEVEMENT

"You have to believe to achieve" is an old saying.

"Anything your mind can conceive and **believe**, it can **achieve**" is a Napoleon Hill saying.

Either or both are the foundation for the achievement of a positive mental attitude.

The formula for
YES!Attitude achievement

I'm about to give you the formula.

It's the same formula that gave me a positive attitude, and that I have followed for the past 35 years. But you must begin with the deep belief that it will happen, or it won't. Believe me, you gotta believe. First.

This formula is real. It's as valid and as true as it can be. And it's delicate. You may perceive it as too simple. Too hokey. You may even say, "I've heard this before." Or, "I just read this."

But, let me state in plain English: **It will work**. I guarantee it will work, but you must believe in yourself, be willing to rededicate yourself, and be willing to *substitute* the negative things you do, for the positive actions you must take to achieve it. If you do, you will not just "get a positive attitude." You will have a *YES!*Attitude for a lifetime.

I have compiled the formula from the pages you have already read. I dripped the elements of the formula to you one by one and have now collected them into a few pages, so you can read and study them in a short space of time and carry them with you until you have achieved.

DECIDE YOU'RE WILLING TO GO FOR IT. Know that the lifelong value of a *YES!***Attitude** is worth it to you. If you can't decide, the rest of the formula is worthless.

DECIDE IT WILL TAKE A YEAR TO SET A NEW THOUGHT PATTERN. A year of positive isn't too long, considering that you have had 30 (more or less) negative ones.

START EACH MORNING WITH SOME POSITIVE EXPOSURE, WISDOM, OR EXPRESSIONS. First thing. Even if your ass falls off. Fifteen minutes, every day.

START YOUR DAY WITH A POSITIVE THOUGHT PROCESS. *I'm happy. It's gonna be a great day. I am the greatest.*

GET RID OF NEGATIVE PEOPLE IN YOUR LIFE. They waste your time and bring you down. If you can't get rid of them (like a spouse or a boss), reduce your time with them.

AVOID THE NEGATIVES. Eliminate negative things and people you come in contact with during the day. Exercise positive choices, and do things that build you up.

AVOID THE VIOLENCE ON TV AND IN MOVIES. Violence generates negative and nervous energy. Violence wastes all your positive energy. Violence begets violence.

IGNORE IDIOTS AND ZEALOTS. When you're on this journey, it may (at times) seem a little silly. *This is a natural feeling.* Stick with it. Hang in there. Let idiots and zealots go their own way. You're on a mission. Let nothing or no one get in your way.

TURN OFF THE TV. Turn off the news (especially the local news). Turn off the weather. (Just look out the window.)

MAKE YOUR OWN ENVIRONMENT. One that makes you happy, gives you peace, and fosters your learning.

READ BOOKS THAT WILL GET YOU GOING AT THE START OF THE DAY. Just a few pages each morning to give you a positive direction, thought, or inspiration. Share what you learned.

LISTEN TO THE RECORDED MESSAGE OF POSITIVE PEOPLE. Their messages will keep you going during the day and in tough times.

SURROUND YOURSELF IN THE EXTERNAL ENVIRONMENTS THAT BREED SUCCESS. Happy, creative, encouraging environments.

CREATE NEW ASSOCIATIONS THAT WILL BOOST YOUR DESIRE TO BE POSITIVE. Happy people, successful people, helpful people.

SMILE ALL THE TIME. Lead with a smile, and the words will follow. Earn a smile from everyone you talk to.

RESPOND TO EVERYTHING IN THE POSITIVE. At first, this requires thought. You MUST stop and think BEFORE you mouth off.

START EVERYTHING IN THE POSITIVE. Tell yourself and others what CAN be done. Tell yourself and others what you WILL do.

SELECT ONE POSITIVE MESSAGE OR ONE PASSAGE. And read it, or listen to it, or watch it every day for a year.

Attitude disciplines and attitude achievement actions
The attitude achievement discipline defined

Your daily exposure to positive or negative information is a choice. Choose to expose yourself to only positive info. Since the news is negative, turn that off! (You'll find you really don't need it.)

NOTE: As I mentioned, avoiding the news does not mean avoiding the *business* news. If there is specific information that you need to succeed in your career, pay full attention to that.

Choose to convert the hour a day that you were wasting watching the news to reading or listening to your personal success library. One hour a day (weekdays) converts to 250 hours in a year (still leaving weekends and a two-week vacation) or more than ten full 24-hour days.

Look at it a different way: If you spend 250 hours watching the news, what will you learn from it that will help you in your career, or with your family, or with yourself? If the answer is nothing, ask yourself the same question about reading books or listening to CDs about your attitude. The answer is everything!

Let's see, you can either have

EVERYTHING

or nothing.

"Hmmm...that's a tough one."

Attitude is reflected in your response to events and your responses to people

When responding to others, most people have what are known as knee-jerk responses. Someone says something to you, and you immediately quip back. Unfortunately, the more you love the person, or the more familiar you are with the person, the more negative the first response tends to be. You've heard of the old expression, "Familiarity breeds contempt."

You are communicating with someone who you know well – brother, sister, friend, wife, husband, mother, father – and you tend to go for the jugular. This would be considered negative.

The sister of negative is cynical, the cousin is satirical, and the mother-in-law is downright abrasive.

BIG SECRET: Maintain a positive environment by formulating your response as a question rather than as a statement.

EXAMPLE: Your employee or co-worker does something wrong. Typically, there will be some gossip or backbiting. And if there's a confrontation, it will predominantly focus on what went wrong, combined with various ass-covering letters or e-mails in the employee file. The guilty employee feels like dirt, is resentful, and shares the same bad attitude that everyone around him or her put out when the deed occurred. The net result of something going wrong at work is poor morale and poor productivity that can last for weeks.

Me? I give the employee one hundred bucks. And then I ask the employee a series of questions that allows them to understand what they did, see their own solution, and keep their dignity.

It's the same way I suggested you be more positive with your children on page 99: Ask them what happened. Ask them if this is the best they could have done. Ask them what they think would have been a better way of doing it. Ask them if they think they can do it a better way the next time. Follow that with "I love you" and a hug.

People don't make mistakes on purpose. The reason I give my employees one hundred dollars is to acknowledge that they were willing to take a risk and fail. The hundred dollars also mitigates any misinterpretation of how, or why, I'm confronting them. My job is to help them succeed, and their job is to feel good about it.

PERSONAL NOTE: I do exactly the same in my office as I do at home. I treat my employees the same way I treat my daughters – with love, respect, and dignity. And when that happens, people look forward to a hug.

Thinking about your problems

Your everyday thoughts and actions build the foundation for the strength of your attitude. If you do the little things with the right attitude, the big things will follow.

Start thinking by reading and writing. Everyone has problems, issues, challenges, and drama in their lives. The difference between positive resolve and negative resolve is the thought process that goes into figuring out the solution.

You've all heard "garbage in, garbage out." Well, it's the same with positive and negative.

When you wake up in the morning, read, write, and contemplate something positive.

The opposite of reading, writing, and contemplating is procrastinating. Procrastination manifests itself in various time-wasters and bad habits, such as watching TV, reading the paper, e-mailing no one special, calling people on the phone for no reason, and other forms of not helping yourself.

ATTITUDE ACHIEVEMENT ACTION: Read something positive for 15 minutes every day. Just read two pages a day. Two pages a day (every day) will give you 730 pages at the end of a year. The key is two pages a day, every day.

When you start your morning by feeding your head with positive, it sets the tone for your productivity and your communication.

But that's not the only learning or thinking you should do. Set aside another four or five hours a week for reading and listening. A few minutes first thing in the morning sets the tone and the pace for the day, but additional reading and thinking reinforces it.

BUSINESS NOTE: You can change the attitude of your entire company by simply selecting the best quote of the morning, one that you read in your two pages. Go in to the office, type it in your computer, make it fancy, acknowledge the author, and e-mail it to everyone on your team.

The first day, everyone will think you're nuts. Do it every day for three weeks. Then skip a day. Everyone will come by your desk and say, "I didn't get my quote. Where's my quote? Is everything okay? Where's my quote?"

ATTITUDE ACHIEVEMENT ACTION: Decide on 365 days as a start for attitude achievement – from today, to a year from today. Use each month as a benchmark of progress. Exchange TV for reading and doing positive things.

Free Git✗Bit: **Want to create an incredible atmosphere in your company?** To find out what a client of mine who employed one hundred people did, go to www.gitomer.com, register if you are a first-time user, and enter the word FRANCE in the GitBit box.

Ultimate attitude achievement action

Take the *YES!***Attitude** formula pages (138-139) and photocopy them.

- **Post them on your bathroom mirror.**
- **Carry them in your pocket.**
- **Read them EVERY morning as you get ready for your day.**

Make the formula and the actions part of your life for one year, and you will win YOUR attitude, not win for others.

If you believe it would help you to do this with others, *carefully* select three or four others to do it with you.

And whatever you do, don't go bragging about what you're doing. For once in your life, **JUST DO IT!**

Drain your brain at the end of each day

"I couldn't sleep at all last night."

That's the first line of the 1958 song, "Tossin' and Turnin'" by Bobby Lewis and one of the biggest laments among salespeople (and regular people). Ever "lose sleep" over a problem or a person? Why?

Stress and worry seem to be major occurrences in life. Got stress? Got worry? *Here are the early warning signals:*

WHINING. Things aren't going right. Wah, wah. (A brother to lamenting: Woe is me.)

WINE-ING. Drinking to forget or drinking to "relax."

COMPLAINING. Looking at what's wrong with things and people.

BLAMING. It's always someone else's fault. "I'd be a millionaire today if it weren't for those other jerks."

CYNICISM. Always a snide remark at the success of others or the condition of the world.

SHORT FUSE. Loose temper that creates negative energy and blocks creative thought.

TYLENOL P.M. A weak excuse as a remedy for "I can't get a good night's sleep."

"Reduce stress" and "eliminate worry" are the wrong philosophies. Converting the *negative* energy of stress to a *positive* energy is the correct philosophy. That way, instead of going to sleep with problems, you go to sleep with peace and a clear mind, and you wake up with solutions.

The stress you have is part of your "struggle" – a natural occurrence in your drive for success. But stress and worry are choices. Your choices. Your mind has thoughts, and they either show up as stress and worry, or you harness the same energy and convert the thoughts into resolve.

Most people lose sleep over matters of unfinished business, money, and passion. **MONEY NOTE:** When money is tight, you will focus on money 30% of the time – or more. When money is not tight, you focus on success and eventually fulfillment.

NOTE WELL: Fulfillment and success are mutually exclusive. There are a *bunch* of successful, unfulfilled (negative) people.

Me? I'm asleep in two minutes or less every night. I wake up refreshed every day. I don't "have to have my coffee" in the morning. I never worry about what I have to do or what loose ends there are. I'm always prepared for the new day, AND I get my best ideas in the morning – writing, reading, walking, jogging, or in the shower. And you can, too!

BIG SECRET: Three words – **Write everything down.**

I keep my laptop (used to keep a legal pad) by my bedside. And the last thing I do before I go to bed is write down everything I need to do or problems I need to resolve. Once I write everything down, my mind is clear.

THE METHODOLOGY IS SIMPLE: Put your problems, your challenges, your obstacles, your goals, and your ideas in writing.

Make small lists such as a:

- **To-do list.** Everything you need to do, big and small.

- **To-call list.** Everyone you need to call, major and minor.

- **To-get over list.** Baggage in your life, empty and full.

- **To-resolve list.** Things that need decision or resolution.

- **To-pay list.** All matters of money you think about, paid and unpaid.

Don't fret over your problems.
Relax so you can get to the solutions.

Then, when you get under the covers, think of past success or past victory. Good times – carefree times – vacations, friends, and all that you are grateful for.

When you do, you will get occasional "thought jolts." Things that are still bugging you that you forgot to write down. **Get back up and write them down.** The secret (of the secret) is to unload *everything*.

When your conscious mind is clear, it provides unobstructed channels from your subconscious mind for solutions and new ideas, and it lets you sleep like a log.

As soon as you wake up, solutions will start to appear. Like magic, your brain will begin to work on your problems in the subconscious, and little ideas will pop into your head. The more you work on the process, the bigger the ideas will be.

Choosing stress is a bad choice.

Choose a pad of paper or a laptop to write everything down at the end of your day. Choose mental freedom. Mental freedom is a wonderful thing. It creates opportunities not available to a cluttered mind.

Write down all the crap, and think of all the good.

Writing is an attitude lesson in disguise. When you write, you express your frustrations and joys to yourself. You expel the frustrations and extol the joys. You release the negative and revel in the positive.

Writing leads to the realization of what you have achieved, how good you are, and what's on the horizon for you to grab and love.

– Jeffrey Gitomer

A WONDERFUL
ALTERNATIVE TO NO!

Adding *YES!* to your positive attitude

Adding **YES!** is the best part of this process. **YES!** is both a way of thinking and a way of speaking. It adds power to attitude. It adds meaning and feeling to attitude. And **YES!** is a way to be certain your meaning is understood.

THINK YES! FIRST: This leads to a **YES!** feeling inside you and a **YES!** response.

Develop the language of **YES!**, even when the answer is (or you're thinking) no. If you give responses that characterize **YES!**, the perception of the recipient will be positive, even though the final resolve may not be **YES!**

To do this requires **YES!** thinking. If you cannot do what is asked of you, or there's a problem that you can't handle, rather than push back or reject the person you're talking to, just say, "The best way to handle that is…" or "The fastest way to accomplish that is…" or "The easiest way to get that done is…"

To respond in terms of **YES!**, you must first think in terms of **YES!** (What can I do? How can I help?) Unfortunately, most people think no first. What they don't understand is the power behind thinking and expressing **YES!** When you saw the phrase, "**YES!** A wonderful alternative to No!" you may have smiled. But this phrase is at the very core of transitioning from no thinking to **YES!** thinking.

5

The reason **YES!** is so powerful is that the recipient of the message is full of hope.

The reason **YES!** is so powerful is that the person delivering the message (that would be you) is FORCED to think of a solution and a way to get things done, rather than just passing the buck, or brushing it off, or telling what can't be done (the easy way out).

The reason **YES!** is so powerful is that it offers a positive atmosphere, a smile, a laugh, a positive expectation, and of course, an agreement of the mind and vocal expression.

Now you know the secret of *YES!* What are you going to do about it?

The secret is so simple, yet 95% of all people fail to do it. Oh, they may "know it." They may have even tried some of the achievement elements at one point in their lives. They may even think they have a great attitude. But they (you) have never studied it, dedicated themselves to it, or applied the principles on a daily basis over an extended period of time.

Now is the time!

You must make the decision that it's worth it to dedicate the time to yourself, the most important person in the world.

You've read the details and now understand what's in it for you. What you can't know before you start is the freedom and peace of mind that positive attitude brings with it:

- **Knowing you have achieved it, and no one can take it away.**

- **Knowing it will always be there with you, to help you weather any adversity.**

Understanding your WHY: the attribute of discovery

There is a critical attitude action of understanding and finding your real positive "why."

ASK YOURSELF:

Why is this important to me?
Why am I doing this?
Why will this help me?

The importance of discovering the right "why" is critical to attitude achievement, because the wrong "why" (doing it for other people or circumstances) may not be powerful enough to achieve attitude.

At the beginning of this book, I stated that attitude is selfish. You do it for yourself. That's your "why" – to be the best person you can be, for yourself FIRST.

To be the best mom, or dad, or husband, or wife, FIRST you must be the best *person*. If you become best for yourself first, you can easily be your best and do your best for others. Achieve attitude for yourself, and the rest of the most important people in your life will benefit forever. I promise.

Understanding your WHEN: the attribute of starting today

Make a plan to do something positive – something for yourself – today and every day for the next year.

It kills me when people delay the start of their life's achievement based on something or someone else.

ATTITUDE ACHIEVEMENT ACTION: Go back to the formula on page 138. List the things that you can begin to do NOW, or just copy the pages and post them in plain view.

This action is step one in making a *visual* commitment to achieve. Seeing what you must do is the best way to keep it top of mind and top priority.

And then there's a matter of keeping it up – maintaining consistency. This is the hardest part of the task, and certainly the acid test that will be delivered over and over as you seek to build attitude strength – and strength of character.

Free Git✗Bit: Consistency is developed, not simply created. **If you're looking for specific examples of how to maintain the habit of consistency that leads to positive attitude, I'll share 3.5 of mine.** Go to www.gitomer.com, register if you are a first-time user, and enter the word CONSISTENCY in the GitBit box.

Understanding your HOW: the attribute of starting with your best thoughts

The easiest way (and time) to realize that attitude is in your head is just before you fall asleep. What do you think about as your head hits the pillow?

I have already told you to drain your brain and write everything down. That helps set the tone and clear your mind. BUT the real win comes when you begin to think about the best times of your life, just before you begin to doze off.

If you fall asleep thinking positive, you'll wake up the same way.

I taught myself that technique in the seventh grade.

Every night, as I was lying in bed trying to fall asleep, I thought about – actually *relived* – those moments all the way through. Vacations, parties, fun times with family and friends. I thought about what I wanted to become and places I wanted to see. Every good, positive thought I could think of.

And I fell asleep almost every night in less than three minutes.

Understanding your *YES!*: the attribute of achievement

YES!Attitude is not just about being a **YES!** person. Nor is it about saying "**YES!**" all the time.

It's not just saying "**YES!**" It's thinking **YES!**, having a **YES!** frame of mind, having a **YES!** outlook on life, and looking at things and people with **YES!** in mind. It's a reinforced way of speaking and taking action.

YES! is not just any thought. *YES!* is your *first* thought.

I believe one of the most interesting aspects of **YES!Attitude** is the inability to define it in a sentence. Like positive attitude, **YES!Attitude** would be defined by one hundred people in one hundred different ways.

Pick your own definition of **YES!Attitude**. But LIVE it; don't just define it.

I believe that **YES!Attitude** follows positive attitude by a year or two. Like any higher form of learning or mental process, you attain mastery over time. Bit by positive bit. Day by positive day. Until one day, it's **YES!**

Morgan spills a *YES!*

This is the best example of **YES!Attitude** to date.

I'm sitting at Einstein Brothers Bagels in Charlotte, having breakfast with my daughter Rebecca, my son-in-law Mike, and two of my beautiful granddaughters, Morgan (8) and Claudia (4).

Morgan reaches across the table and with one motion spills her milk all over everything. She looks at what she has done and exclaims, "First spill of the day!"

I was howling. I was ecstatic. She said it naturally, as though it was part of her being, not just a casual thought.

Morgan is a positive kid. Her parents are positive people. And her grandfather sets the standard. Attitude rubs off and is passed down – especially familial attitude. Kids mimic parents and other family members from admiration, not just respect.

YES! comes from your soul, not just your mind.
YES! comes from your heart, not from your lips.
YES! is first a thought from a mindset – then it's a word.

You have to think **YES!** before you can say it. When your mindset is right, the rest flows naturally.

Think **YES!** first.
The rest that follows will be positive.

Is there a turning point?
Is there a beginning point?
YES! And they are
the same point.

There was a day when I realized that I had achieved attitude – that nothing was going to get in my way, and that I was ready to face the world and win.

But I can't tell you what day that was. It snuck up on me. And I was past it before I realized it had happened. I was acting the part of having a positive attitude for so long that it just took over naturally and became part of my inner being.

When you study attitude *daily*,
when you live the principles of it *daily*,
and when you dedicate the *daily* time
to achieve your positive attitude, it just
takes over, and you don't realize
it until you see yourself manifesting
it in your words and actions.

Here's how I got mine...

How I got my attitude.
Fake it till you make it: myth or must?

Here's how I achieved my positive attitude, my **YES!Attitude.**

How I sold myself on how important it was.
How it was the biggest and best sale I ever made.
And what was happening while I struggled to get it.

My mother's brother was a doctor. That automatically made my mother a doctor, and she wanted me to be a doctor. But I wanted to be a businessman, like my dad.

I started my own company in 1969 making leisure furniture and beanbag chairs in Camden, New Jersey. I had the gift of gab, but I never really understood the science of selling.

My business rolled along with moderate success, I took on a partner, and there was added pressure to increase sales.

One day, in early 1972, two friends of mine came over to my place and started to tell me (sell me) about this multilevel marketing company called Dare to Be Great. Something about Glenn Turner. Something about mink oil. Something about *if somebody puts in two thousand, I get one thousand.*

can't really remember the details, but if you've ever seen the movie *The Bank Dick,* starring W.C. Fields, it was like the famous scene where J. Frothingham Waterbury (Russell Hicks) sells Egbert Sousé (W.C. Fields) 5,000 shares in the "Beefsteak Mines" in Leap Frog, Nevada, for ten cents a share. Don't get me started...I know the whole scene by heart. It's one of the best sales pitches in movie history.)

My friends ended their sales rant by telling me, "You're going to get a positive attitude, you're going to learn how to sell, and you're going to make big money. Go, go, go!"

So I sold my business to my partner, and I took up with this group of Glenn W. Turner, Dare to Be Great zealots. And every day, from eight in the morning until noon, ten guys sat in a room and took a sales lesson and a positive attitude lesson. Four hours a day, every day, for one year.

We read and studied books like *Psycho-Cybernetics, The Magic of Thinking Big, How to Win Friends & Influence People,* and *A Message to Garcia.* We watched the movie (yes, a 16MM movie) called *Challenge to America* at the beginning of each training session – a twenty-minute, Glenn W. Turner film in which he closes the 2,000 people in his audience all at once. It's *the* sales-cult classic film of all time.

We learned from and listened to all of the masters of selling from that time (J. Douglas Edwards, Bill Gove, Herb True, Zig Ziglar, Fred Herman, and others) using the brand new technology of cassette tapes.

But our bible was Napoleon Hill's classic, *Think and Grow Rich*. Each person was responsible for writing and presenting a book report on one chapter each day. There were 16 chapters in the book, 10 people in the room, and we did this for one year. You can do the math for how many times I have read the book. I was also exposed to 10 other people's opinion of the book – 10 other people who were on fire and seeking to attain the same dream.

We created our own language. Problems were called "temporary situations." Obstacles were called "attitude checks." Negative people were called martians.

I think it's only fair to tell you, that at the same time I was trying to get this positive attitude, my then wife was pregnant with the twins, the marriage was bad, my funds were limited, and from a career perspective, I had no real goal or direction.

My life was less than stellar. I had no money and no direction. BUT I was studying positive attitude every day.

Friends would ask me how
I was doing, and I would
extend my arms into the
air and scream, "Great!"

Even though I was crappy.

was not positive yet. But I knew that by acting it and exuding it, eventually I would attain it. I wanted that positive attitude, bad. Every day, I would come in to work and face the cassette player with my spiral notebook. And as Earl Nightingale was bellowing advice, I was taking notes and looking at the machine as though it were alive. I was determined to turn my study into reality.

ONE OTHER THING YOU SHOULD KNOW: Every friend of mine thought I was nuts. You see, not only did I watch the movie *Challenge to America* five times a week at the office, but I would also take it (and the projector) home on the weekends and play it for my friends. They were convinced that I had lost my mind. I was convinced that I was finally taking control of it.

One day I woke up, and I had a positive attitude. I don't know what day it was, but I can clearly recall that I was going to let nothing get in my way, no matter what life threw at me. I was determined that I was going to take my newfound mental wealth and convert it into real wealth.

I also became a lethal weapon of selling. I could persuade using a combination of the science of selling, my passion to be the best, my passion for life, and my intelligence.

I immersed myself in the study and the "living example" of positive attitude. You could say I "faked" it, but that's a weak definition. What I was doing was "living it in advance." And I did that until I actually "got it." I GOT IT! I GOT IT!

FAST FORWARD A FEW DECADES: Have I kept it? Or should I say, "How have I kept it?" or "How have I maintained it?"

Life happens. And often there's little or nothing you can do about it. But I make my own positive attitude happen during life.

I've had bad days and experienced bad events like anyone. Death of parents, relationship splits, low money, no money, broke, flat broke, bankruptcy, rejection, making big mistakes, throat operation, and other regular doses of life.

"You can learn a lot about success by failing a few times."

– Max Gitome
1919-1998 (my father

No matter what has happened to me, for more than three decades, my attitude has been set on positive – always there to kick-start my ass to get over it, and move ahead.

Setbacks, challenges, and other "attitude checks" are reality. And reality is the test of attitude strength. When I went broke, my positive attitude kicked in to remind me, "temporary situation."

ATTITUDE ACHIEVEMENT RULE: Immerse yourself in positive attitude thoughts, words, people, and actions every day, and a positive attitude will be yours. I promise.

If you think that I'm nuts, you may be right.

But I'm a nut with a positive attitude, baby.

5

How to maintain your attitude

You've all heard the phrase, "The squeaky wheel gets the oil." But no one ever addresses how the wheel got squeaky in the first place. **ANSWER:** Rust, lack of use, or misuse.

ATTITUDE MAINTENANCE RULE: Reinforce your attitude every morning. Talk to yourself. Read to yourself. Write to yourself.

What did you do this morning to build your attitude? (Probably nothing, or not enough.)

Me? I read something positive every day. Just a few pages every morning. I've only been doing it for 35 years. I'm going to do it for another 35 years, and then that's it. I'm gonna quit.

Let me take attitude maintenance deeper

PREVENTIVE ATTITUDE MAINTENANCE IS:

- Reading something positive every morning.
- Thinking positive thoughts every morning.
- Having an attitude sanctuary to think and decompress.
- Saying positive things every morning.
- Knowing your direction BEFORE you start walking.

PRACTICE ATTITUDE MAINTENANCE IS:

- Random acts of positive attitude.
- Random acts of kindness.
- Saying positive things all day long.

URGENT ATTITUDE MAINTENANCE IS:

- People confronting you.
- Arguments.
- Life's crap.

REJUVENATIVE ATTITUDE MAINTENANCE IS:

- Looking at how kids act.
- Listening to how kids talk.
- A walk in the park.
- Talking to a friend.
- Reading a positive book.
- Listening to your favorite music.

The 15-minute first thing in the morning *YES!*Attitude drill

Many people wake up in the morning and do push-ups. They exercise their body muscles.

BRAIN-UPS: This drill is about exercising your mental muscles, more specifically, your thinking muscle – your attitude muscle.

These actions get you thinking in the right direction:

1. **Create positive thoughts.**
2. **Read positive thoughts.**
3. **Write positive thoughts.**
4. **Think and plan positive actions for the day.**
5. **Speak positive words to yourself and others.**

5.5 **Ignore all bullshit.**

Taking the right actions
first thing in the morning
sets the tone for
the rest of the day.

All students of attitude need renewal

Writing is the fulcrum point of my thinking and my attitude.

Since I began writing a weekly column about sales, service, loyalty, attitude, and personal development in March of 1992, my whole world changed.

Writing has helped create legacy and fortune for me. And I did it without a goal. I never started out to be a writer. I started writing, and the rest just happened.

The book you are reading is my seventh.

Writing this book has reinforced my attitude. It has helped me discover new ideas and has made me rediscover some of the joys of the past – both failed and successful.

And the same can happen to you. Just start!

Free Git✗Bit: Think you're not a good writer? Or have you just not written enough or practiced enough? Like all elements of life, there are guidelines that will help you write better, or should I say "write right." **Want my personal list of writing guidelines?** Go to www.gitomer.com, register if you are a first-time user, and enter the words WRITE RIGHT in the GitBit box.

ATTITUDE FULFILLMENT

Fulfillment is
the difference
between inspiration
and motivation.

Attitude is not
"motivating."
It's "inspiring!"

There's a BIG difference between success and fulfillment

I know a ton of VERY successful people who are miserable, or better stated, unfulfilled. They're successful and unhappy, maybe cynical, resentful, or even worse, bitter.

My dad was successful, but bitter. He started out happy, but over the years, he became more and more critical of others who couldn't (or didn't) see it his way. Other people never cared what they did to him and cared even less what my dad thought of them. It was a valuable lesson for me: Don't get bitter, get better – and get over it.

The benefits of a lifelong *YES!Attitude* are internal happiness, gratefulness, and thankfulness. Fulfillment begins with extended internal happiness, combined with a love of what you do, and a pride of accomplishment and achievement – the inner glow of self-assurance that creates an outward, peaceful aura.

Fulfillment is wanting more but being content and at peace with what you have – being internally, and eternally happy, regardless of circumstance or the people involved.

What is the value of a lifetime of inner positive attitude and happiness? It cannot be measured in dollars. That's the best part. You determine the value of fulfillment, and you discover the worth – and the wealth – every day.

Both positive attitude and **YES!Attitude** breed positive anticipation that's a strategic advantage in your career, especially in sales. With my attitude, I assume I will make every sale I attempt. I assume I am going to get a "Yes." And I assume both before I begin the presentation. It's fulfilling, especially when I walk out with a check.

BUT THE REAL QUESTION IS: What is fulfillment to you? Achieving the highest level in the field you love? Retiring in Florida? (For some, it's Sarasota. For me, it would be Boca Raton.) Paying off your mortgage and becoming debt free? Seeing your book in print? (That was a pretty fulfilling moment for me.)

Well, whatever it is, attitude will lift it to the heights you are hoping for.

Fulfillment is not a one-time thing you get at the end of the rainbow. Fulfillment happens all the time. It's about personal accomplishment, being proud of a family member's achievement, doing something you love to do, or helping others achieve their hopes and dreams.

Attitude fulfillment comes from sustaining it. It comes from having to call on your attitude in a time or need or crisis, and it's there for you. Attitude is fulfilling when it lifts you up in personal tragedy or helps you through health issues.

Attitude fulfillment helps you see money when none is there. And it helps you through too much self-indulgence, if you have it and want to lead a life of clear thinking, or a smoke-free one.

Attitude fulfillment helps you when your spouse, parents, or children are in need of love and support. And it helps you encourage them rather than chastise them.

I have always looked at my attitude as a gift. A gift I gave myself. I have always looked at my attitude as a blessing. A blessing I gave myself.

"What's the best way to find a better attitude, eBay or Google?"

What kind of freedom can a *YES!* Attitude bring?

Mental freedom. The freedom to think and create that only exists when a positive attitude is present – and prevalent.

In the beginning of this book, I talked about getting into an argument with someone and five minutes later calling to mind what you wish you would have said in the heat of the argument. And the lesson was "negative blocks creative."

That was an easy one for you to understand because it has happened to you a hundred times.

To gain fulfillment, you have to take that understanding a lot deeper and realize what it does to you at the critical moments of decision making and responding.

Many people have petty arguments on "big days" because emotions are running at their highest level, and that's when a person's real feelings, or real attitude, comes forward.

Probably the easiest one to recognize is on a wedding day. Arguments, crying, regretting the decision – even calling off the wedding – are more of a result of attitude than they are of argument. In other words, the argument was enabled because the attitude was negative.

Think about your family life, your business life, your personal life, and your social life. And think about the responses that you've had to other people and the actions that you've taken when your feelings were negative or your mindset was negative. Most of those actions, most of those responses, are both regretted and regrettable.

I'm not saying, "Live the perfect life, think the perfect thoughts, and everything will be rosy." I'm not saying, "You have to be positive 100% of the time, or you'll never find the pot of gold at the end of the rainbow."

I am saying, "Be aware of your internal feelings and your internal thoughts before you make a response, or before you commit an action that, in retrospect, you could've avoided."

You'll know when these occur less than one minute later, as you begin to profusely apologize, grovel, eat dirt, and feel anywhere from inadequate to pathetic. You've done it. I've done it. Everyone on the planet has done it.

The key to fulfillment is working on being aware of it more and doing it less. This is one of the most difficult disciplines because other people and other things are interacting with your thought process and challenging it.

Unfortunately, the first response is not to be benevolent. The involuntary response tends to be both defensive and argumentative. That's the real world. Your job, as the master of your own attitude, is to create a personal calm before responding to a negative situation. The more you do it, the more you will feel fulfilled.

Come on, Billy. Walk to Mommy!

The same way you encourage a one-year-old baby to walk and the same way you celebrate a one-year-old's birthday are the best ways to understand how your attitude should be toward people and life. Encourage and celebrate.

You can't remember the day you took your first step. And you can't remember the overindulgent party that ensued on your first birthday.

But what stayed with you were the remembrances of the praise that you received and the love that you received, that were consistent throughout learning to walk and celebrating that first birthday.

I'm challenging each of you to treat everyone like a one-year-old. Just drop the baby talk.

The lost secret of achievement that everybody already knows: encouragement.

The more you encourage people, the more you feel fulfilled. The more you praise people, the more you feel fulfilled. The more you thank people, the more you feel fulfilled *and* the more thankful you become.

There IS a Santa Claus!

Think there's no Santa Claus? You couldn't be more WRONG.

Wake up, Rudolph! **YOU are Santa Claus.**

You make your list. *You* check it twice. *You* go to the store and buy everyone's presents to put under the tree. Parents, siblings, spouses, children, business associates, friends, and even "have to" people, all receive Christmas gifts from *You*, Santa.

Think of all the Santa Clauses in the world. Hundreds of millions of people who are Santa Claus and have no concept of their title, much less their power. Especially when it comes to what you can do with your power on every other day *but* Christmas.

If you're Santa Claus, you can make Christmas any day you want. Why not today? And instead of buying everybody else presents, go get yourself one. Go to Nordstrom and buy yourself something big. Buy yourself something expensive. Buy yourself something you've always wanted. Or buy yourself something fun, just for the hell of it. You can do it – you're Santa Claus.

I'm not saying to go overboard. I am saying, *treat yourself to the gratification and fulfillment of giving yourself things that make you feel good.*

I explained earlier that attitude achievement is selfish, and selfish is okay with respect to attitude. Being Santa Claus gives you the perfect opportunity to give yourself gifts that make you feel great about who you are and to create the environment that will encourage you to achieve the goals you've set for who you want to become.

It may not be a gift from Nordstrom (although that's a good start), but it may be a membership to a health club, or a course that you enroll in at your local community college, or a vacation that you have always wanted to take. Whatever it is that's on your personal Christmas list, put yourself at the top of it. Create your own feeling of success that enables you to do the things for yourself that you want to do for others – without feeling that it's a sacrifice.

Being your own Santa Claus creates a success environment, both mental and physical. When I went to New York to get my first book, *The Sales Bible*, published (a big sale for me) in 1993, my personal funds were limited. I had to borrow money to go make the sale.

I checked around for hotels that were relatively inexpensive. I asked my friend, Mitchell Kearney, where to stay, and he said, "Don't think cheap. Think best!" and recommended I stay at the Royalton Hotel at 44 West 44th Street. He told me that writers and media people stay there, that the hotel was cool, that I would love it, and that it would make me feel great to stay there.

He was right.

When I walked into the Royalton and glanced to my left in he lobby, there was Pete Townsend sitting on a couch. (For hose of you under 30, Pete Townsend was the lead guitar player for The Who, and he was in New York City at the time producing the Broadway play *Tommy.*) I knew I was in the right place.

I gave myself "the gift of first class." Every day, as I was getting dressed to hit the streets to sell my book, I made certain that I looked first class, acted first class, and talked first class. And after 13 first-class rejections, I got one first-class **YES!**

Santa Claus had delivered again, and it wasn't the night before Christmas.

"*What do you mean you've never slid down a chimney?*"

Just before you take your last breath, spend your last nickel

HINT: Don't just leave money, leave a legacy.

Leave things and acts that helped or inspired others, and you will live forever in the hearts and minds of those you have served.

That's leaving a legacy of *YES!*Attitude.

And you can quote me on that!

Think about the quotes you have read and the quotes you have kept that have inspired you. Many of them you have pasted onto your wall. Many of them you have forwarded on to others.

I challenge you to create your own.

Free Git✗Bit: I have collected tons of *great* attitude quotes over the years – everyone from Albert Einstein to Oscar Wilde. **Want my collection of attitude quotes for your personal inspiration?** Go to www.gitomer.com, register if you are a first-time user, and enter the words ATTITUDE QUOTES in the GitBit box.

Your *YES!*Attitude
is permission…

A ***YES!*Attitude** is your ability to think, listen, speak, and react in a positive way.

Your ***YES!*Attitude** is permission…

To see the good in things, not the bad.

To see how to make bad things good.

To see the opportunity and the resolve when an obstacle faces you.

To see things from the *what is right* side, not the *what is wrong* side.

To treat others the way you want to be treated.

To encourage others when they need support.

To never let the negative things affect you for more than five minutes.

To (almost) never have a "bad day."

To have something nice or humorous to say.

To be internally happy.

To work at maintaining your attitude every day.

When you can replace "To" with "I" and add "all the time" at the end of each sentence, then you've got a ***YES!*Attitude**.

If not, read this book again, study it, put it into practice, and decide and commit that you want to win for life – that you will do whatever it takes to make it happen for yourself.

Gitomer's Affirmations of *YES!*Attitude Success

Here are 25 things you can tell yourself each morning to get the direction you really need, and affirm that you're as cool as you think you are:

- I am the friendliest person in the world.

- I am the most enthusiastic person in the world.

- I am the most helpful person in the world.

- I will tell myself what I can do, not what I can't.

- I love to serve.

- I love to sell.

- I don't prejudge or put down anyone.

- I will take control of myself and my success.

- I will remember the good times as often as I can.

- I will ask for what I want.

- I will stick at it until I win, even if my ass falls off.

- Life may not be a blast right now, but look at all I've learned, and look where I can get with hard work.

- I will reinforce my decisions with positive thoughts, not negative second guesses.

- I will thank everyone for their help and never measure.

- I will ask before I tell.

- I will give with pride.

- I will be memorable.

- I will avoid arguments.

I will not gripe or whine about my lot in life. Rather, I will celebrate all I have, all I love, and all I will learn.

- I will feel GREAT when I make a sale.

- I will earn more when I make the sale.

- I will celebrate my victories today.

- I am grateful for life and living.

- I will have a great time tomorrow.

- I will *get over it* in less than one minute and get back to enjoying life.

The rule of every day

The words "every day" appear in this book 46 times for a reason. Or, should I say that "every day" is *the* reason.

If you are going to achieve positive – if you are going to achieve **YES!** – then "every day" is the guiding light, the yellow brick road, the golden gate, the one-way path, the ultimate answer, and the only answer – combined into one.

Every day is also the MAJOR CLUE, the ATTITUDE ACTION, and the KICK IN THE ASS.

It's the answer to achieving AND maintaining **YES!Attitude**.

Looking for the secret? The magic potion? The force behind your personal power?

Just give yourself a dose of positive attitude every day!

Once you figure out that attitude is a gift and a blessing, it is my hope that you give it to yourself and you bless yourself, forever.

— Jeffrey Gitomer

Attitude...pass it on

When my daughter Rebecca was in the seventh grade, she was asked to write her autobiography. She wrote a four-page document that captured "the moment" more than the historical evolution.

Like my other daughters, Erika and Stacey (twins), Rebecca lives in the present. Or should I say, "in the moment." Rebecca is the mother of two (also daughters) to Morgan and Claudia. To complete the all-girls team, Stacey has a daughter, Julia. All girls, all the time.

Rebecca, my youngest by six years, was the first mother of the three. At 19 years of age, she transformed from irresponsible to ultimate responsible in one minute – the minute she saw the ultrasound ticker and realized she was about to become a mother.

Her turnaround earned the respect of her heretofore rivals, her twin sisters.

Rebecca has blossomed as a mother. Her positive attitude was always inside of her, but when Morgan was born, her attitude solidified and has remained steadfastly positive to a point that I have admired it every time I witness it.

Here's a paragraph from her autobiography that she wrote when she was 11-years-old:

...Now I'm going to tell you what kind of person I am. I'm a pretty nice person and a very friendly one.

One really good thing about me is I'm a very positive person (just like my dad)...

**A positive attitude,
a *YES!*Attitude, isn't just
something that you have.
A positive attitude,
a *YES!*Attitude, is something
you can share with someone
that you really love.**

**Tonight, sit around your
dinner table and share your
*YES!*Attitude with someone
that you really love.**

– *Jeffrey Gitomer*

Attitude library bibliography

There is a long list of authors who have positively influenced my attitude and my way of thinking.

Napoleon Hill. Orison Swett Marden. Dale Carnegie.
Russell Conwell. Elbert Hubbart. Norman Cousins.
Ayn Rand. Maxwell Maltz. David Schwartz. Robert Collier.
Charlie "Tremendous" Jones. W. Clement Stone. Ian Falconer.
Albert Einstein. Earl Nightingale. Watty Piper. Dr. Seuss.

NOTE: I am not listing their book titles on purpose. Discover *your* attitude, not mine. Think *your* way, not mine. Go on your own mission. Hunt down their books. Create your own personal development library.

ATTITUDE ACTION: Carry a positive book around with you. When you get a spare moment, read a page or two.

"People do not realize the immense value of utilizing spare minutes."

– Orison Swett Marden
from his book, *He Can Who Thinks He Can!* (1908)

Hey, I said,
"GET OVER IT!"

Attitude slump?
Bad attitude day?
Bad attitude moment?
Reality bite you – in the ass?

If you really want to understand what achievement of attitude is about, the biggest action you can take is "Get over it!"

- **Things in life test your attitude.**

- **Bad service tests your attitude.**

- **Traffic tests your attitude.**

- **Weather tests your attitude.**

- **People test your attitude.**

- **Arguments test your attitude.**

- **Life tests your attitude.**

- **The gods test your attitude.**

THE SECRET IS: Get over it – as fast as you can.

Regroup by taking a walk, reading a page, petting your pet, having a cup of tea, diverting your mental attention toward something you love to do (for me, it's collecting baseball cards and sports memorabilia), or calling your best friend just to shoot the breeze (but don't start moaning).

CHALLENGE: How fast can you move on, get over it, and forgive after something negative happens?

If you can get over any event, confrontation, or person in less than five minutes, you're on the right path – the *YES!*Attitude path. If you can get over it in less than two minutes, you're there.

NOTE WELL: Negative drains *twice* as much energy from your body *and* your soul as positive. Better stated: negative takes energy – positive builds it.

YES! maintains energy and keeps it moving forward.

So, if a secret to *YES!*Attitude lies in the way you get over the shit of life, what can you do about it? Why can't you recover faster and move on?

You can! Practice getting over it, every day. The most common attitude moments are arguments, petty fights, and misunderstandings at home and work. Forgive and forget in five minutes or less. Don't just move on. Move up!

Me? I smile. In one second. No matter what.

An attitude of gratitude

Thank you to my editor, assistant, secret weapon, and best friend, **JESSICA MCDOUGALL**. She devoted herself to this book and it shows. To merely call her an editor is almost a disservice. Her ability to challenge my word choice, refine graphic placement, understand my voice, and work with everyone in the communication chain from the graphic designer to the printer is excellent – and gratefully acknowledged.

Thank you to a new graphic designer for us, **MIKE WOLFF**. He took a stab at this one and did a GREAT job. Mike was rapid to respond, eager to learn our style, and able to adapt his talent to our needs.

Thank you to my brother **JOSH GITOMER**, who designed the cover and added his graphic excellence to the body of text. Josh has the sense of what works, and his cover alterations, combined with his taste, have given the book the added "kiss."

Thank you to my **ATTITUDE MENTORS** – in person, in books, and on tape – who transferred their knowledge and their wisdom to a willing – nay, EAGER – student.

Thank you to my **FAMILY** for manifesting the attitude I have tried to be an example of, rather than a teacher of.

Thank you to **YOU**, my customer who, by purchasing my books, acknowledges and confirms my purpose and legacy. I am grateful and will continue to work hard and write real, to earn your loyalty and support.

JEFFREY GITOMER
Chief Executive Salesman

AUTHOR. Jeffrey is the author of *The New York Times* best sellers *The Sales Bible* and *The Little Red Book of Selling*. All of his books have been #1 best sellers on Amazon.com, including *Customer Satisfaction Is Worthless, Customer Loyalty Is Priceless, The Patterson Principles of Selling, The Little Red Book of Sales Answers*, and his latest book, *The Little Black Book of Connections*.

OVER 100 PRESENTATIONS A YEAR. Jeffrey gives seminars, runs annual sales meetings, and conducts live and Internet training programs on selling and customer loyalty. He has presented an average of 120 seminars a year for the past ten years.

BIG CORPORATE CUSTOMERS. Jeffrey's customers include Coca-Cola, D.R. Horton, Caterpillar, BMW, BNC Mortgage, Cingular Wireless, MacGregor Golf, Ferguson Enterprises, Kimpton Hotels, Enterprise Rent-A-Car, AmeriPride, NCR, Stewart Title, Comcast Cable, Time Warner Cable, Hilton, Liberty Mutual Insurance, Microsoft, BlueCross BlueShield, Principal Financial Group, Wells Fargo Bank, Carlsberg Beer, Baptist Health Care, Wausau Insurance, GlaxoSmithKline, Northwestern Mutual, MetLife, Sports Authority, AC Neilsen, IBM, The New York Post, and hundreds of others.

IN FRONT OF MILLIONS OF READERS EVERY WEEK. Jeffrey's syndicated column, "Sales Moves", appears in more than 95 business newspapers worldwide and is read by more than four million people every week.

SELLING POWER LIVE. Jeffrey is the host and commentator of *Selling Power Live*, a monthly, subscription-based sales resource bringing together the insights of the world's foremost authorities on selling and personal development.

ON THE INTERNET. Jeffrey's WOW! Web sites www.gitomer.com and www.trainone.com get as many as 25,000 hits a day from readers and seminar attendees. His state-of-the-art Web presence and e-commerce ability has set the standard among peers and has won huge praise and acceptance from customers.

TRAINONE ONLINE SALES TRAINING. Online sales-training lessons are available at www.trainone.com. The content is pure Jeffrey – fun, pragmatic, real-world, and immediately implementable. TrainOne's innovation is leading the way in the field of customized e-learning.

SALES CAFFEINE. Jeffrey's weekly e-zine, *Sales Caffeine*, is a sales wake-up call delivered every Tuesday morning to more than 130,000 subscribers, free of charge. This allows him to communicate valuable sales information, strategies, and answers to sales professionals on a timely basis.

SALES ASSESSMENT ONLINE. The world's first customized sales assessment, renamed a "successment," will not only judge your selling skill level in 12 critical areas of sales knowledge, it will also give you a diagnostic report that includes 50 mini-sales lessons. This amazing sales tool will rate your sales abilities and explain your customized opportunities for sales knowledge growth. The program is aptly named KnowSuccess because *you can't know success until you know yourself.*

AWARD FOR PRESENTATION EXCELLENCE. In 1997, Jeffrey was awarded the designation of Certified Speaking Professional (CSP) by the National Speakers Association. The CSP award has been given less than 500 times in the past 25 years and is the association's highest earned award.

Buy Gitomer, Inc.

310 Arlington Avenue, Loft 329, Charlotte, North Carolina, 28203
www.gitomer.com   704/333-1112   yes@gitomer.com

Turn the *Little Gold Book* into your GOLD!

Jeffrey's *Little Gold Book of YES!Attitude* is available as a blended learning solution.

A **YES!Attitude** is 100% responsible for the success of your people, and the success of your business, and no one has ever taken a course in it.

Here's your chance:

Jeffrey's *Little Gold Book of YES!Attitude* packaged training contains facilitator guides, participant workbooks, multimedia support, job aids, and e-learning reinforcement.

Call 704/333-1112 and scream,

"More *YES!*"

Other titles by Jeffrey Gitomer

THE LITTLE BLACK BOOK OF CONNECTIONS
(Bard Press, 2006)

THE LITTLE RED BOOK OF SALES ANSWERS
(Pearson Prentice-Hall, 2006)

THE LITTLE RED BOOK OF SELLING
(Bard Press, 2004)

CUSTOMER SATISFACTION IS WORTHLESS, CUSTOMER LOYALTY IS PRICELESS
(Bard Press, 1998)

THE SALES BIBLE
(John Wiley and Sons, 2003)

THE PATTERSON PRINCIPLES OF SELLING
(Lito Press, 2006)